HOW TO DRAW CARTOON CHARACTERS FOR CREATIVE KIDS

ABOUT THE AUTHOR.

DAVID HAILWOOD HAS BEEN ACTIVE IN THE UK COMICS INDUSTRY FOR OVER 20 YEARS, CONTRIBUTING TO SUCH TITLES AS EGMONT'S BEST SELLING CHILDREN'S COMIC **'TOXIC'**, **HOTCHPOTCH**, AND **100% BIODEGRADABLE.** HE HAS ALSO WORKED AS A SPECIAL SKILLS TUTOR, TEACHING FILM, ART, AND COMIC MAKING TECHNIQUES TO CHILDREN ACROSS THE SOUTH COAST OF ENGLAND.

www.davidhailwood.com

How To Draw Cartoon Characters For Creative Kids is published by Biomekazoik Press (biomekazoik@gmail.com).

SECTION ONE
CREATE YOUR CHARACTERS

ALPHABEASTS

'A' SHAPE
ADD EYES, NOSE, EARS AND TEETH
TOENAILS
1
'B' SHAPE
DRAW EYES, MOUTH AND EARS
ADD AN ARM
1
DRAW FURRY ARMS
2
ADD A TAIL
DRAW CLAWED FEET
2
ADD FUR TO LEGS
3
GIVE IT A BELLYBUTTON
3
DRAW YOUR OWN HERE!

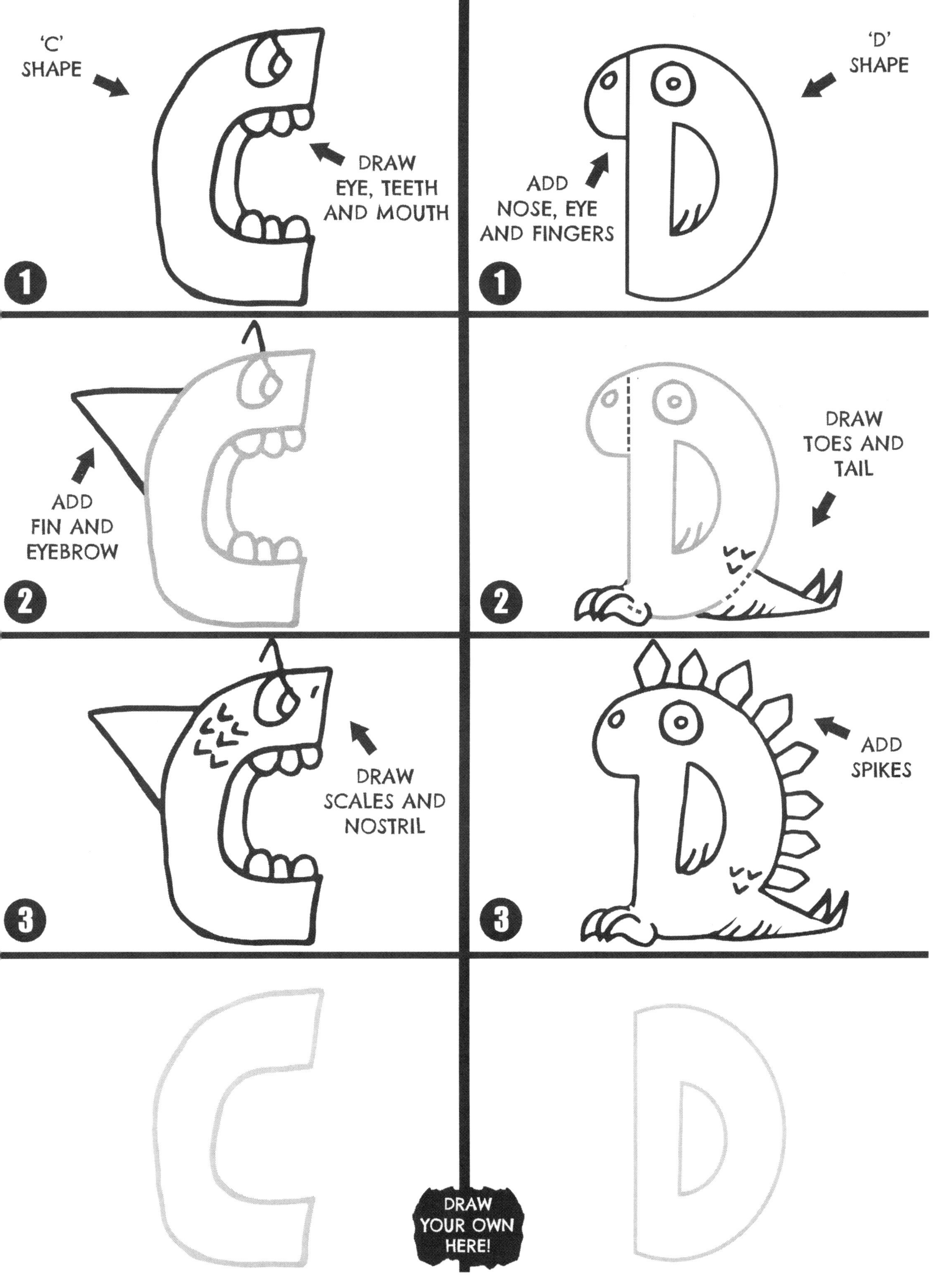
'C'
SHAPE
DRAW
EYE, TEETH
AND MOUTH
1
'D'
SHAPE
ADD
NOSE, EYE
AND FINGERS
1
ADD
FIN AND
EYEBROW
2
DRAW
TOES AND
TAIL
2
DRAW
SCALES AND
NOSTRIL
3
ADD
SPIKES
3
DRAW
YOUR OWN
HERE!

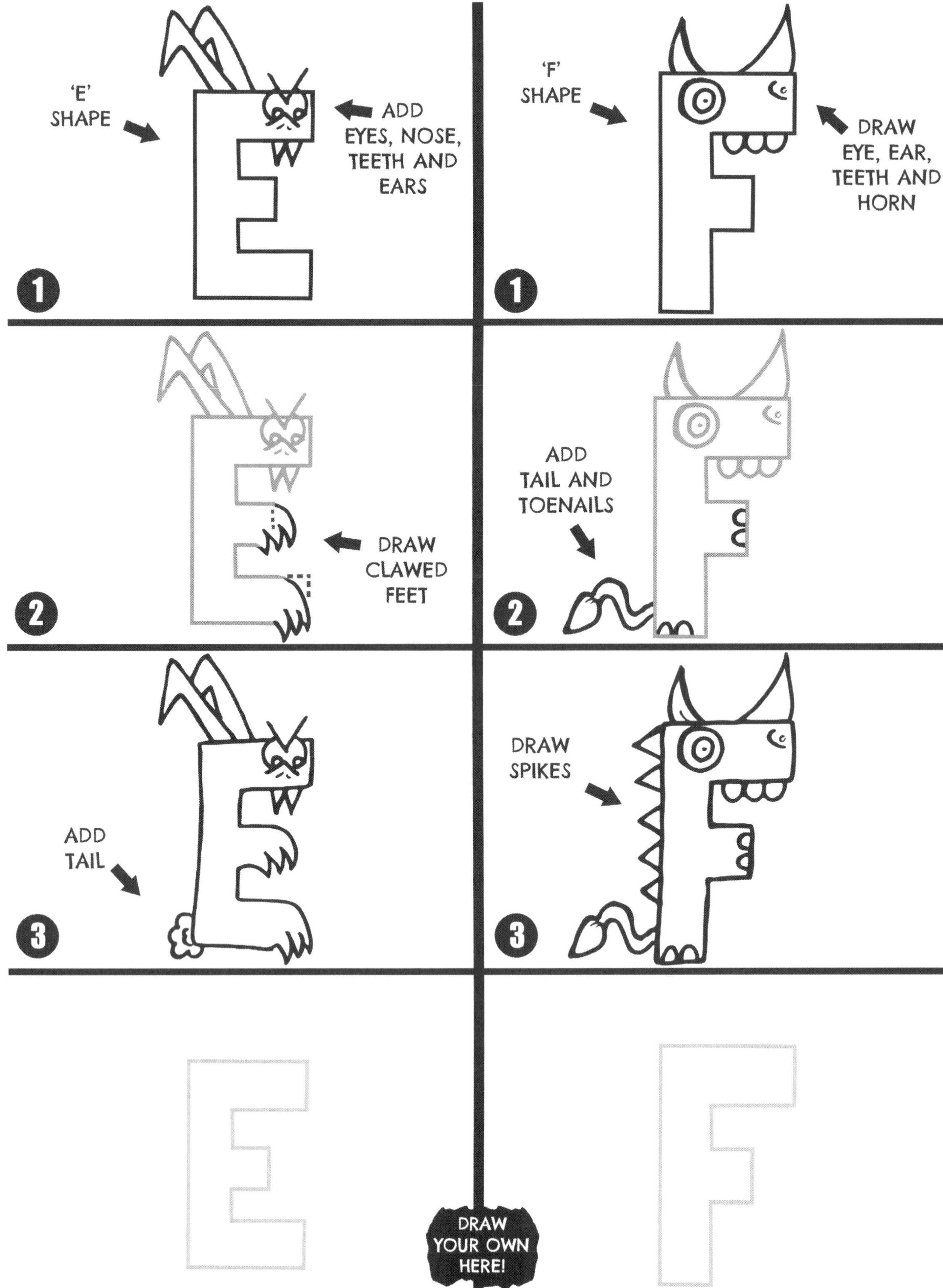
'E' SHAPE
ADD EYES, NOSE, TEETH AND EARS
1
'F' SHAPE
DRAW EYE, EAR, TEETH AND HORN
1
DRAW CLAWED FEET
2
ADD TAIL AND TOENAILS
2
ADD TAIL
3
DRAW SPIKES
3
DRAW YOUR OWN HERE!

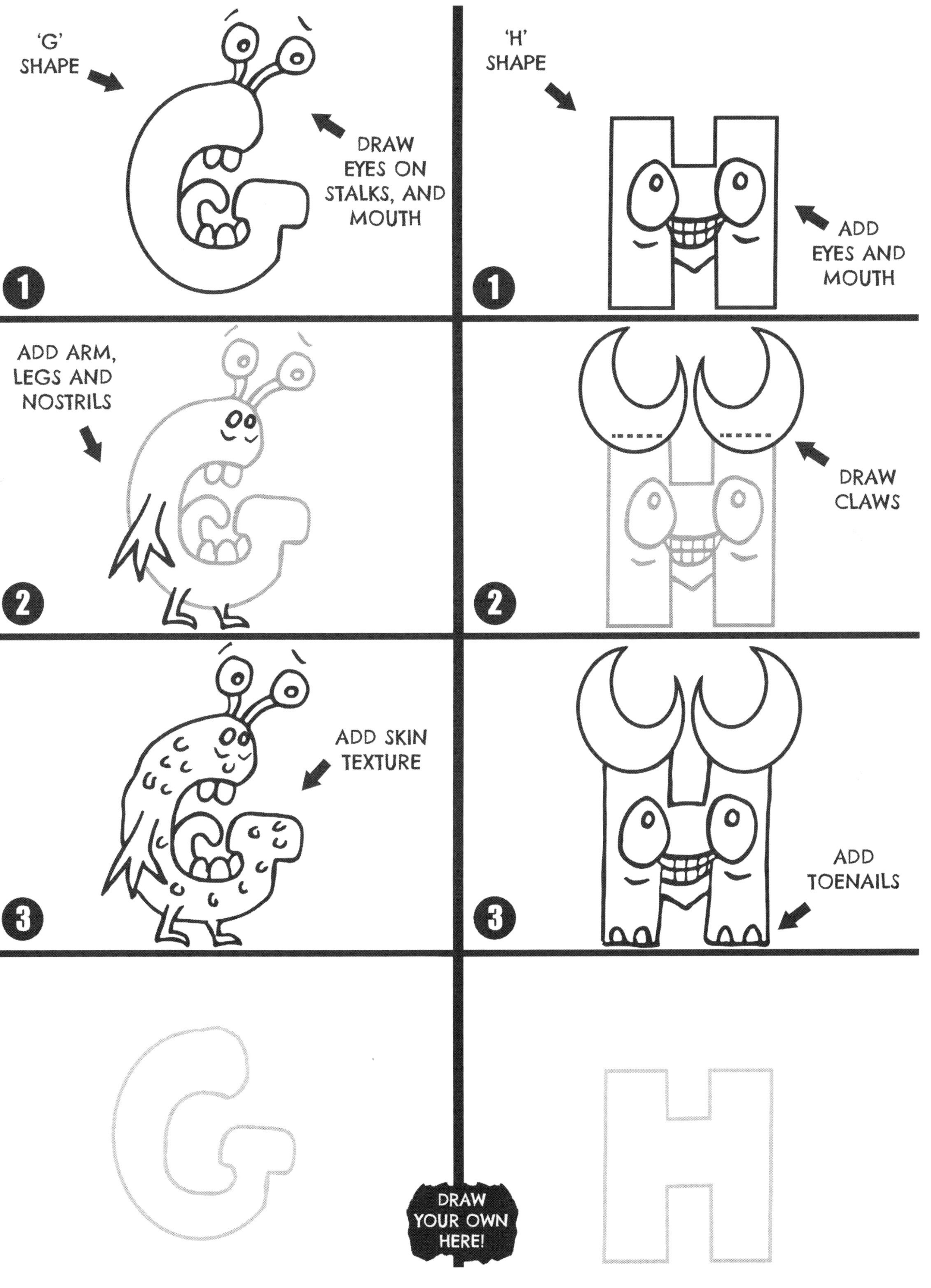
'G' SHAPE
DRAW EYES ON STALKS, AND MOUTH
1
'H' SHAPE
ADD EYES AND MOUTH
1
ADD ARM, LEGS AND NOSTRILS
2
DRAW CLAWS
2
ADD SKIN TEXTURE
3
ADD TOENAILS
3
DRAW YOUR OWN HERE!

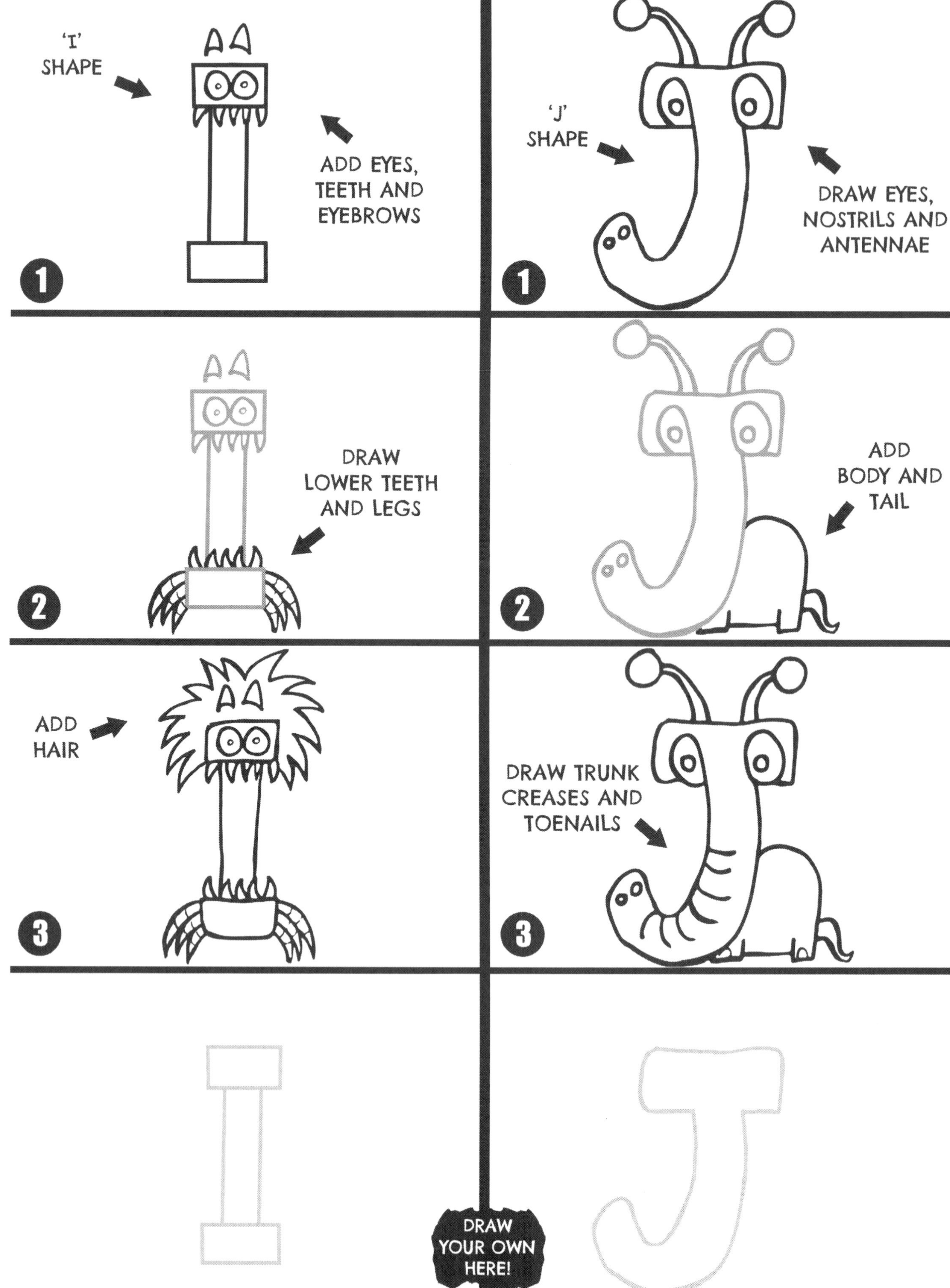
'I'
SHAPE
ADD EYES,
TEETH AND
EYEBROWS
1
'J'
SHAPE
DRAW EYES,
NOSTRILS AND
ANTENNAE
1
DRAW
LOWER TEETH
AND LEGS
2
ADD
BODY AND
TAIL
2
ADD
HAIR
3
DRAW TRUNK
CREASES AND
TOENAILS
3
DRAW
YOUR OWN
HERE!

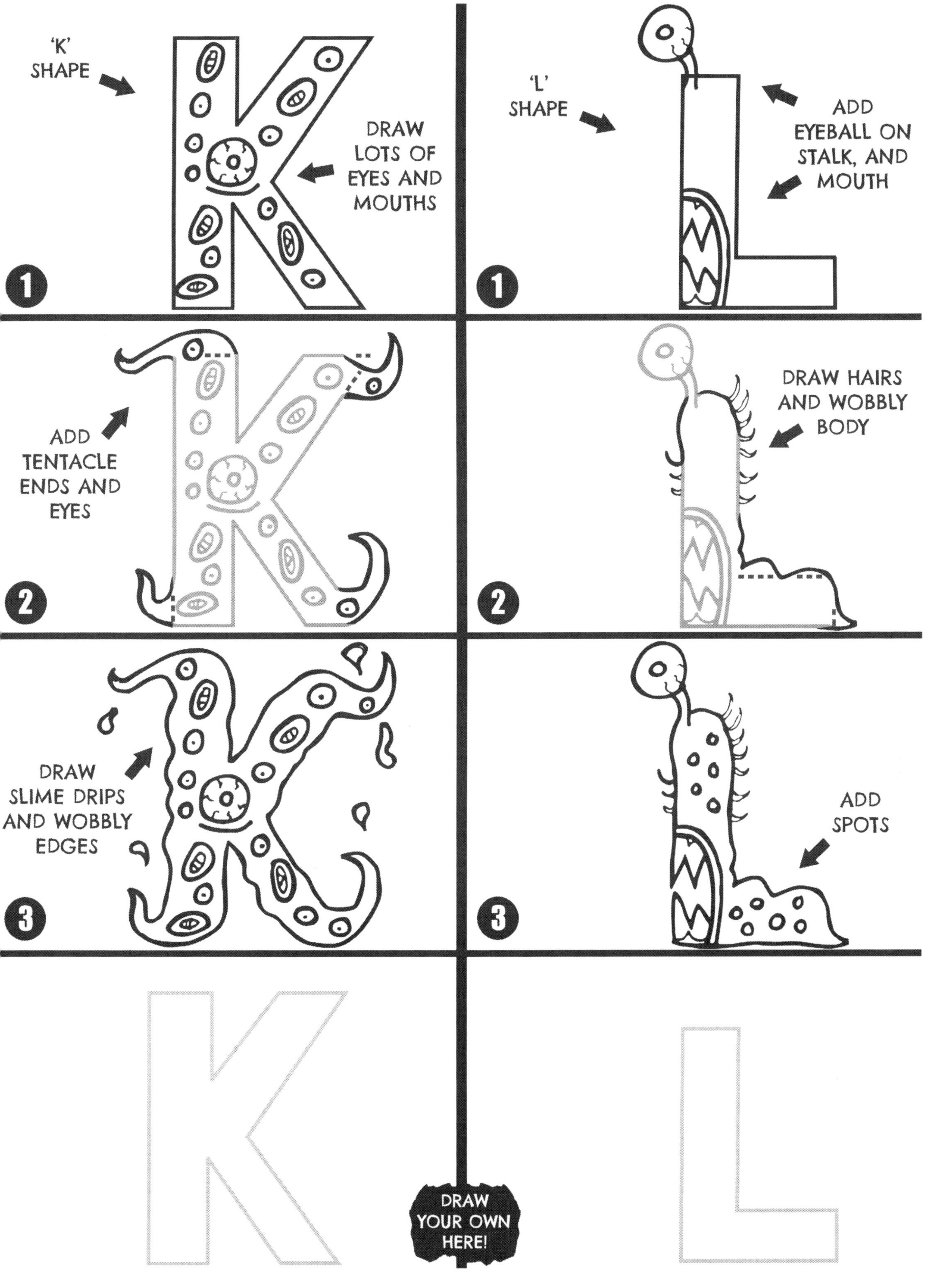
'K' SHAPE
DRAW LOTS OF EYES AND MOUTHS
1
'L' SHAPE
ADD EYEBALL ON STALK, AND MOUTH
1
ADD TENTACLE ENDS AND EYES
2
DRAW HAIRS AND WOBBLY BODY
2
DRAW SLIME DRIPS AND WOBBLY EDGES
3
ADD SPOTS
3
DRAW YOUR OWN HERE!

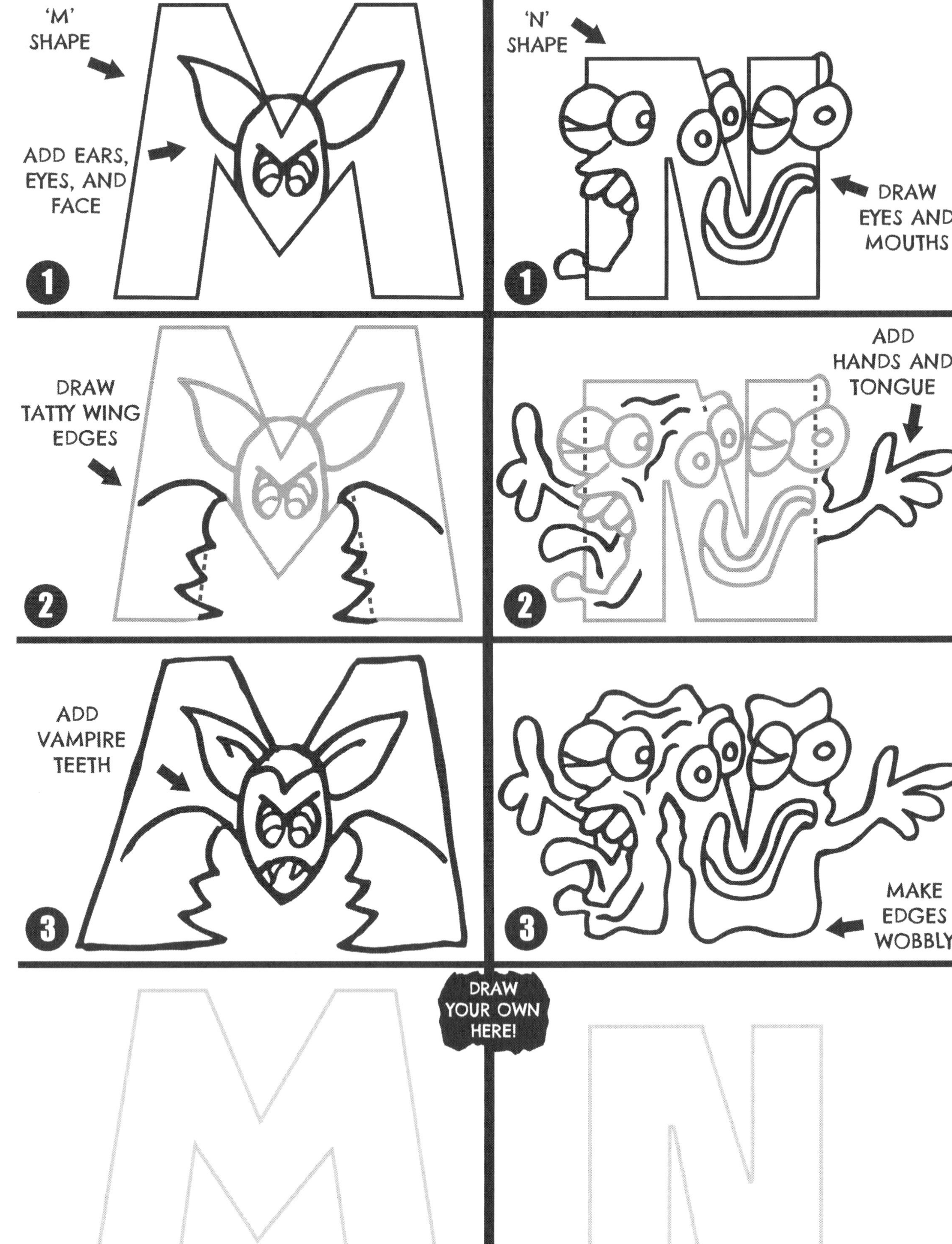
'M' SHAPE
ADD EARS, EYES, AND FACE
1
'N' SHAPE
DRAW EYES AND MOUTHS
1
DRAW TATTY WING EDGES
2
ADD HANDS AND TONGUE
2
ADD VAMPIRE TEETH
3
MAKE EDGES WOBBLY
3
DRAW YOUR OWN HERE!

'O'
SHAPE
ADD
TENTACLES
1
'P'
SHAPE
DRAW
ARMS, FOOT
AND TAIL
1
DRAW
TENTACLE
EYES
2
ADD
EYES AND
NOSTRILS
2
ADD
MORE
EYES!
3
DRAW
TEETH AND
CHIN SPOTS
3
DRAW
YOUR OWN
HERE!

DRAW
HORN AND
EYEBALL
'Q'
SHAPE
1
ADD
EYE, NOSE,
MOUTH AND
BEARD
'R'
SHAPE
1
ADD
WINGS, TAIL
AND ARM
2
DRAW
EARS AND
HOOFS
2
DRAW
A MOUTH
3
ADD
ARM AND
HOOF
3
DRAW
YOUR OWN
HERE!

'S'
SHAPE
DRAW
EYE, NOSTRIL
AND TEETH
1
'T'
SHAPE
ADD
EYES, NOSE
AND MOUTH
1
ADD
BODY AND
ARM
2
DRAW
ARMS
2
DRAW
SPIKY HAIR
3
ADD
WAVY
HAIR
3
DRAW
YOUR OWN
HERE!

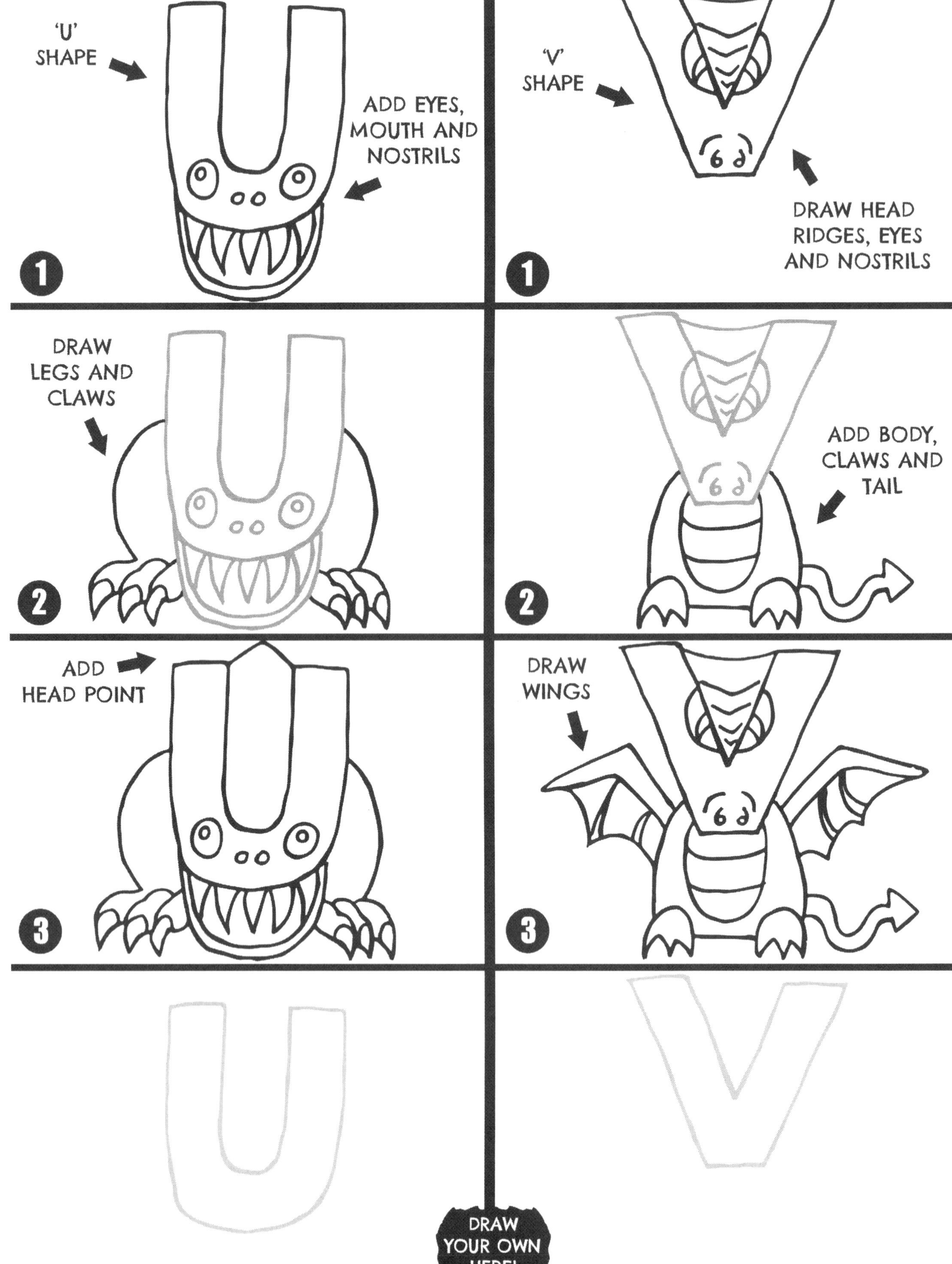
'U' SHAPE
ADD EYES, MOUTH AND NOSTRILS
1
'V' SHAPE
DRAW HEAD RIDGES, EYES AND NOSTRILS
1
DRAW LEGS AND CLAWS
2
ADD BODY, CLAWS AND TAIL
2
ADD HEAD POINT
3
DRAW WINGS
3
DRAW YOUR OWN HERE!

'W' SHAPE
DRAW EYES, NOSE AND FACE
1
'X' SHAPE
ADD EYES, MOUTH AND FACE FUZZ
1
ADD EARS, MOUTH AND LEGS
2
DRAW HAIR, TEETH AND FEET
2
DRAW HANDS AND TEETH
3
ADD TAIL AND NOSTRILS
3
DRAW YOUR OWN HERE!

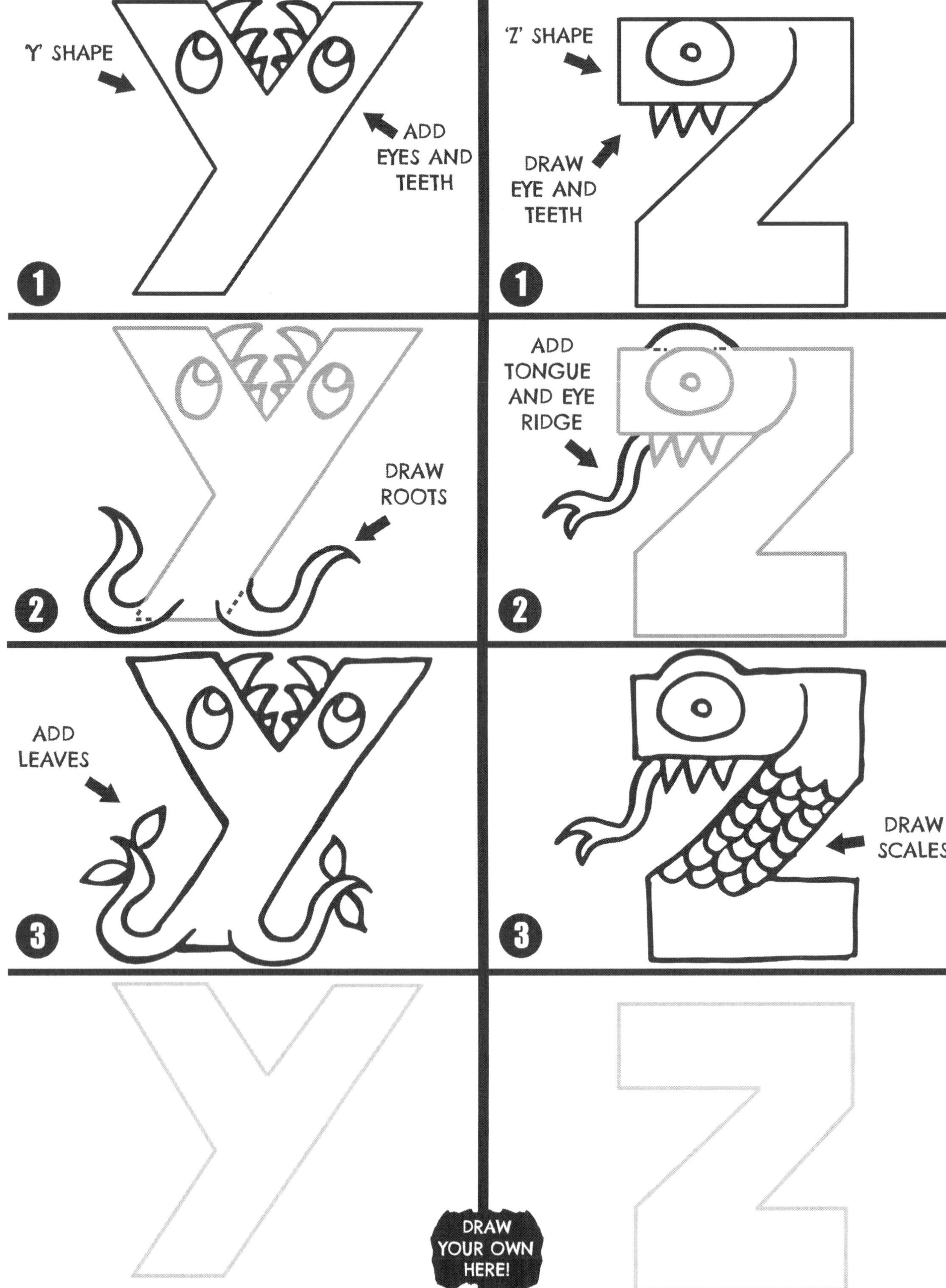
'Y' SHAPE
ADD EYES AND TEETH
1
'Z' SHAPE
DRAW EYE AND TEETH
1
DRAW ROOTS
2
ADD TONGUE AND EYE RIDGE
2
ADD LEAVES
3
DRAW SCALES
3
DRAW YOUR OWN HERE!

ALPHA
BOTS

'A' SHAPE
DRAW EYES AND TEETH
1
'B' SHAPE
ADD EYE AND NOSE CANNON
1
ADD ARMS AND FEET
2
DRAW ANTENNA AND WHEELS
2
DRAW ANTENNAE
3
ADD TRACKS
3
DRAW YOUR OWN HERE!

'C'
SHAPE
DRAW
FACE, EYES
AND MOUTH
1
'D'
SHAPE
ADD
EYES AND
TEETH
1
ADD
ARM AND
LEGS
2
DRAW
ARMS
2
DRAW
TRIANGLE
AND CIRCLE
ON HELMET
3
ADD
WHEEL
3
DRAW
YOUR OWN
HERE!

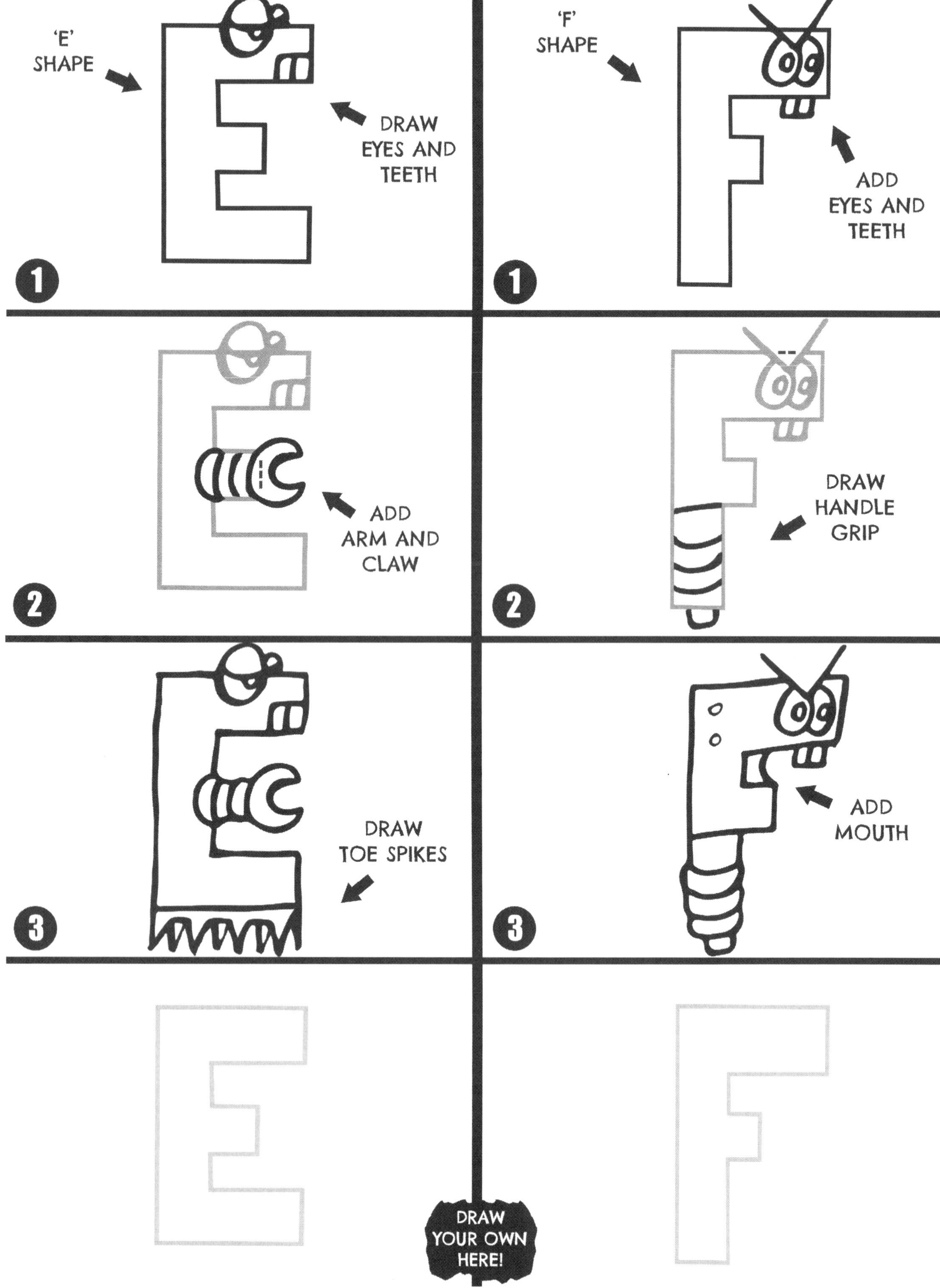
'E'
SHAPE
DRAW
EYES AND
TEETH
1
'F'
SHAPE
ADD
EYES AND
TEETH
1
ADD
ARM AND
CLAW
2
DRAW
HANDLE
GRIP
2
DRAW
TOE SPIKES
3
ADD
MOUTH
3
DRAW
YOUR OWN
HERE!

'G' SHAPE
DRAW EYES AND TEETH
1
'H' SHAPE
ADD EYES AND EYEBROWS
1
ADD EYEBROWS AND SIGHTS
2
DRAW MOUTH
2
DRAW BODY SEGMENT LINES
3
ADD ARMS
3
DRAW YOUR OWN HERE!

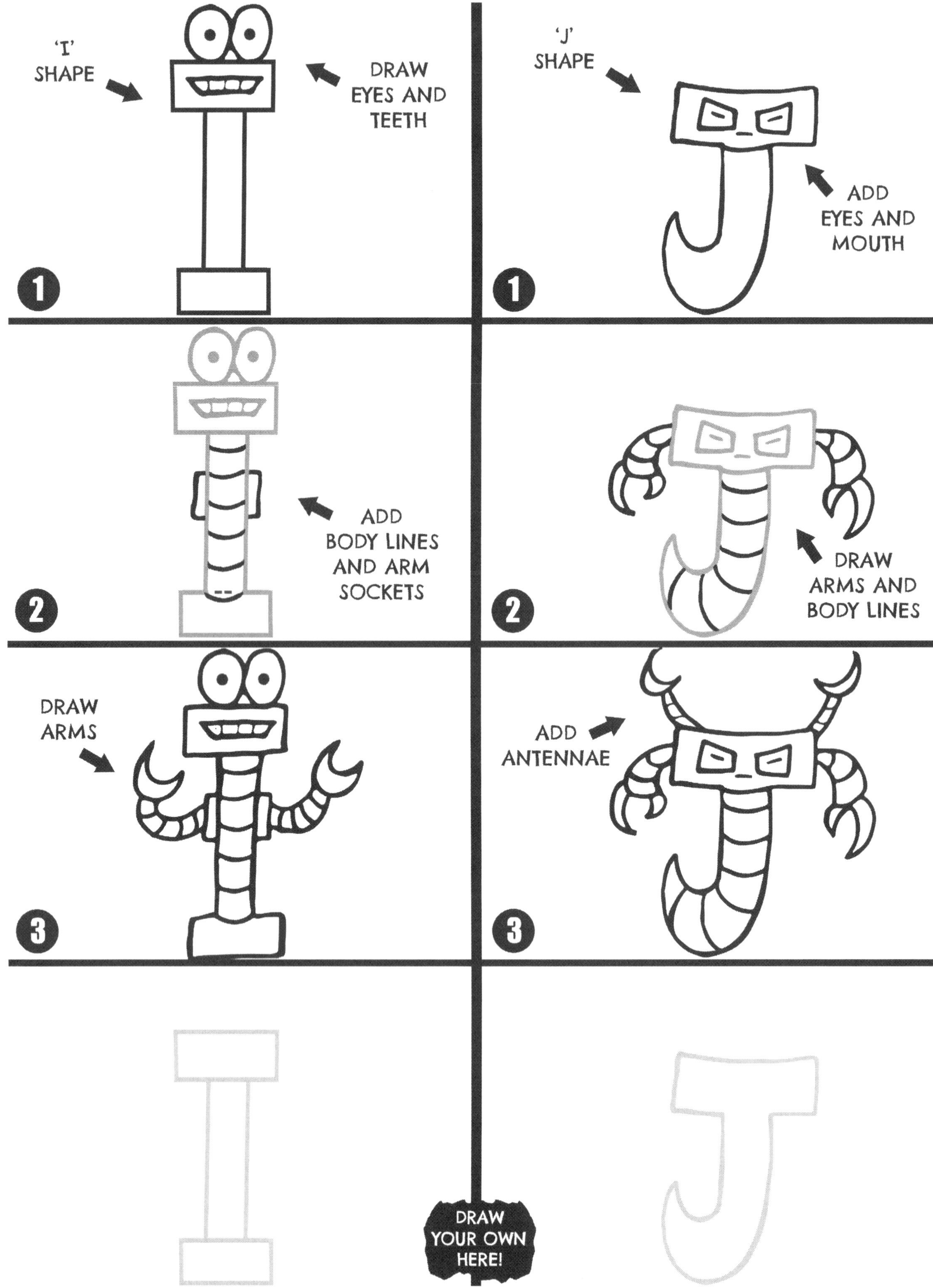
'I'
SHAPE
DRAW
EYES AND
TEETH
1
'J'
SHAPE
ADD
EYES AND
MOUTH
1
ADD
BODY LINES
AND ARM
SOCKETS
2
DRAW
ARMS AND
BODY LINES
2
DRAW
ARMS
3
ADD
ANTENNAE
3
DRAW
YOUR OWN
HERE!

'K'
SHAPE
DRAW
EYE AND
MOUTH
1
'L'
SHAPE
ADD
EYES AND
MOUTH
1
ADD
NOSE CANNON
AND FEET
2
DRAW
ARMS
2
DRAW
ARMS
3
ADD
TRACKS AND
WHEELS
3
DRAW
YOUR OWN
HERE!

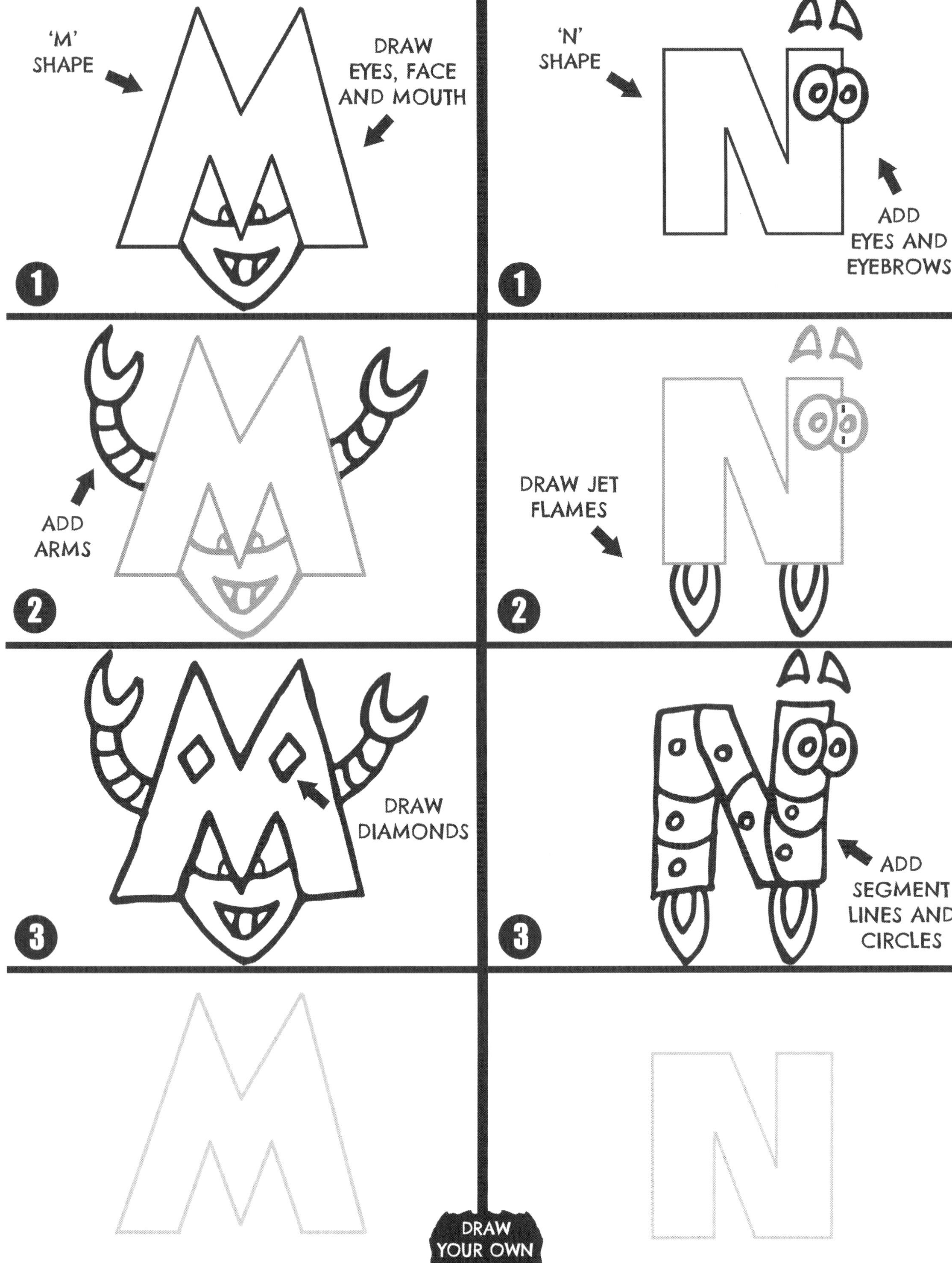
'M' SHAPE
DRAW EYES, FACE AND MOUTH
1
'N' SHAPE
ADD EYES AND EYEBROWS
1
ADD ARMS
2
DRAW JET FLAMES
2
DRAW DIAMONDS
3
ADD SEGMENT LINES AND CIRCLES
3
DRAW YOUR OWN HERE!

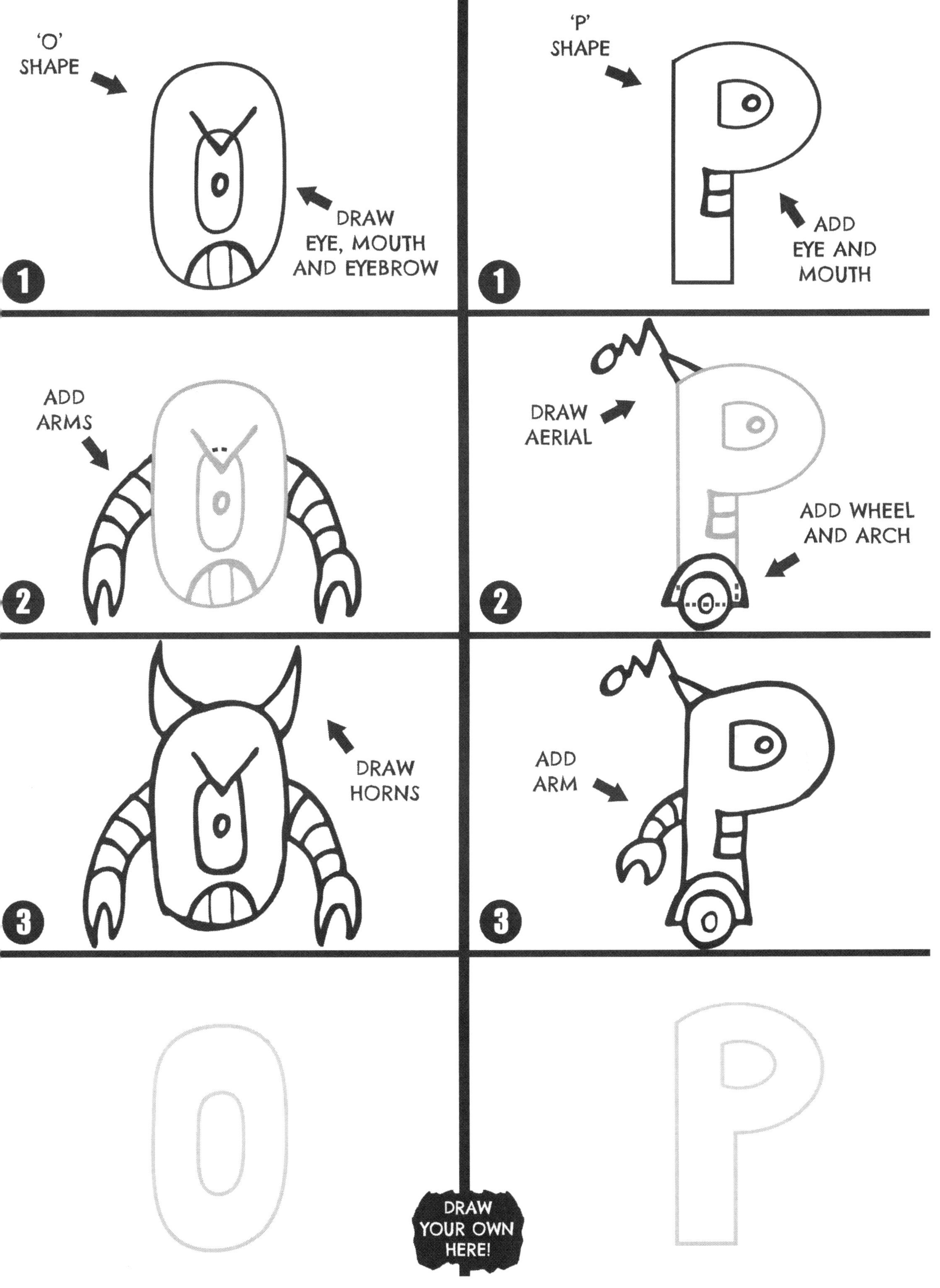

'O'
SHAPE
DRAW
EYE, MOUTH
AND EYEBROW
1
'P'
SHAPE
ADD
EYE AND
MOUTH
1
ADD
ARMS
2
DRAW
AERIAL
ADD WHEEL
AND ARCH
2
DRAW
HORNS
3
ADD
ARM
3
DRAW
YOUR OWN
HERE!

'Q' SHAPE
DRAW EYEBALL ON A STALK
1
'R' SHAPE
ADD EYES AND MOUTH
1
ADD ARM AND JET FLAME
2
DRAW ARMS
2
DRAW SHELL SWIRLS
3
ADD FEET
3
DRAW YOUR OWN HERE!

'S' SHAPE
DRAW AN EYE
1
ADD ANTENNAE AND TAIL
2
DRAW BODY SEGMENTS AND CIRCLES
3
'T' SHAPE
ADD EYES, MOUTH AND FACE
1
DRAW ARMS AND LEGS
2
ADD DIAMONDS
3
DRAW YOUR OWN HERE!

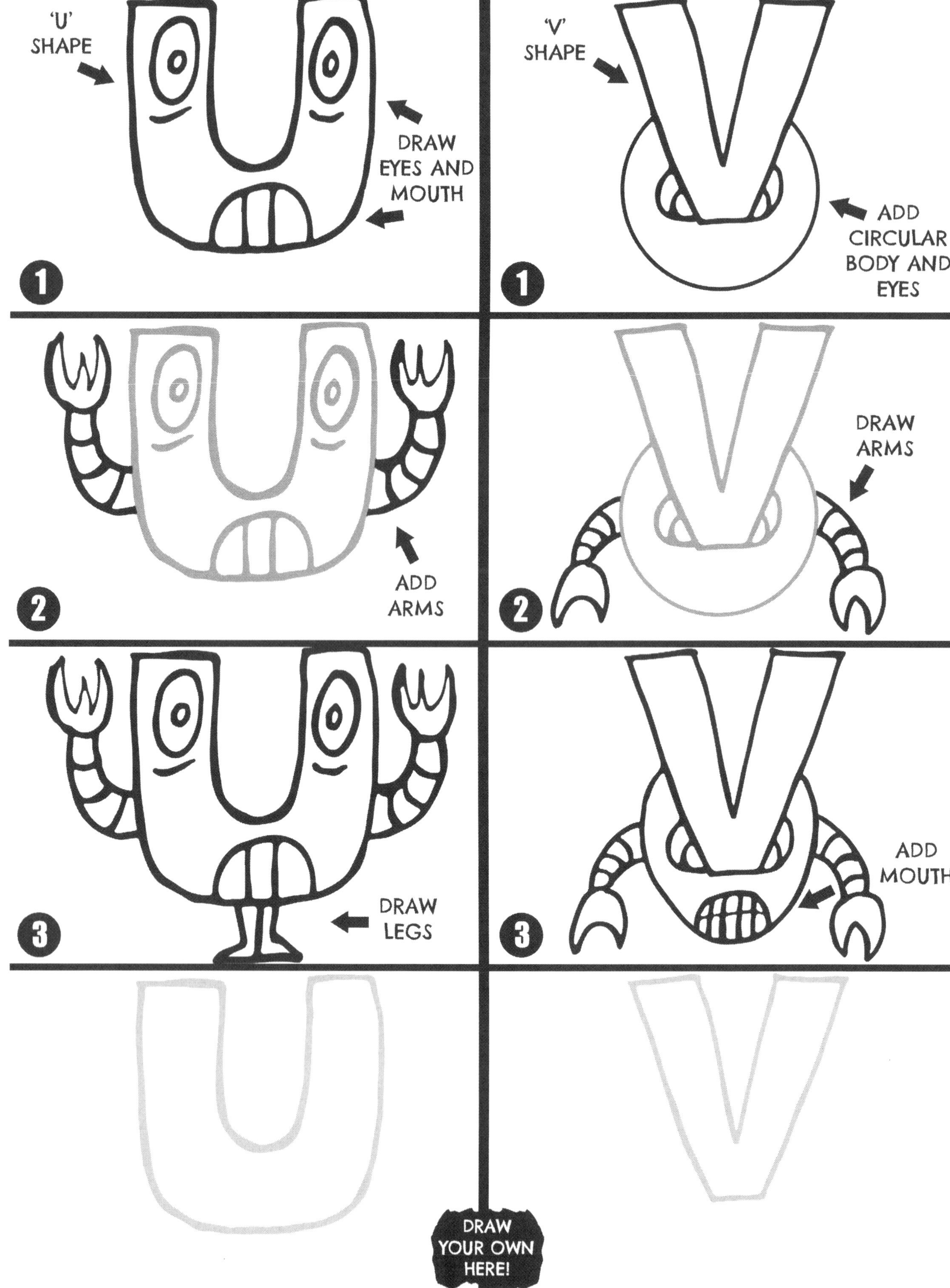
'U' SHAPE
DRAW EYES AND MOUTH
1
ADD ARMS
2
DRAW LEGS
3
'V' SHAPE
ADD CIRCULAR BODY AND EYES
1
DRAW ARMS
2
ADD MOUTH
3
DRAW YOUR OWN HERE!

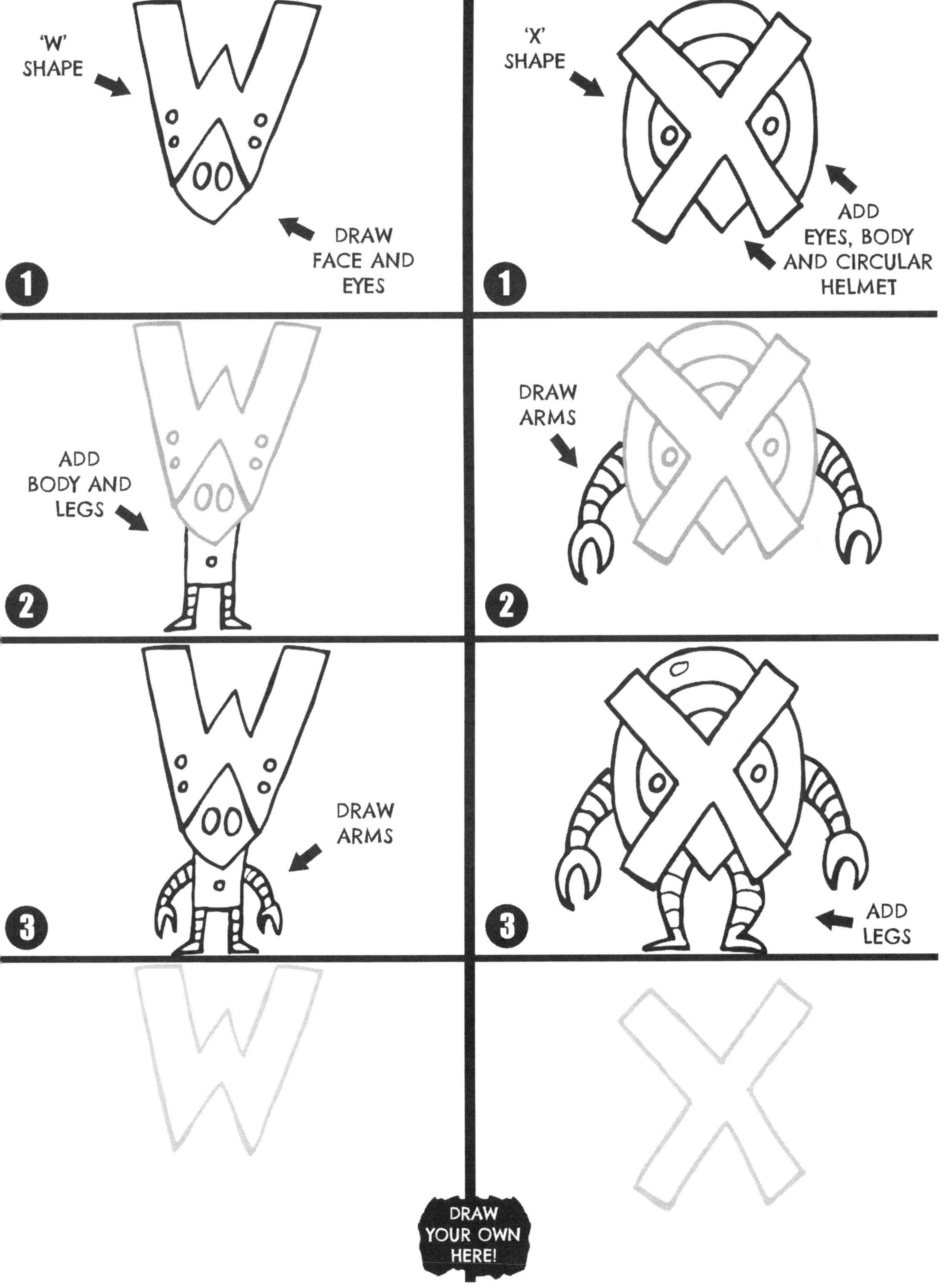
'W' SHAPE
DRAW FACE AND EYES
1
'X' SHAPE
ADD EYES, BODY AND CIRCULAR HELMET
1
ADD BODY AND LEGS
2
DRAW ARMS
2
DRAW ARMS
3
ADD LEGS
3
DRAW YOUR OWN HERE!

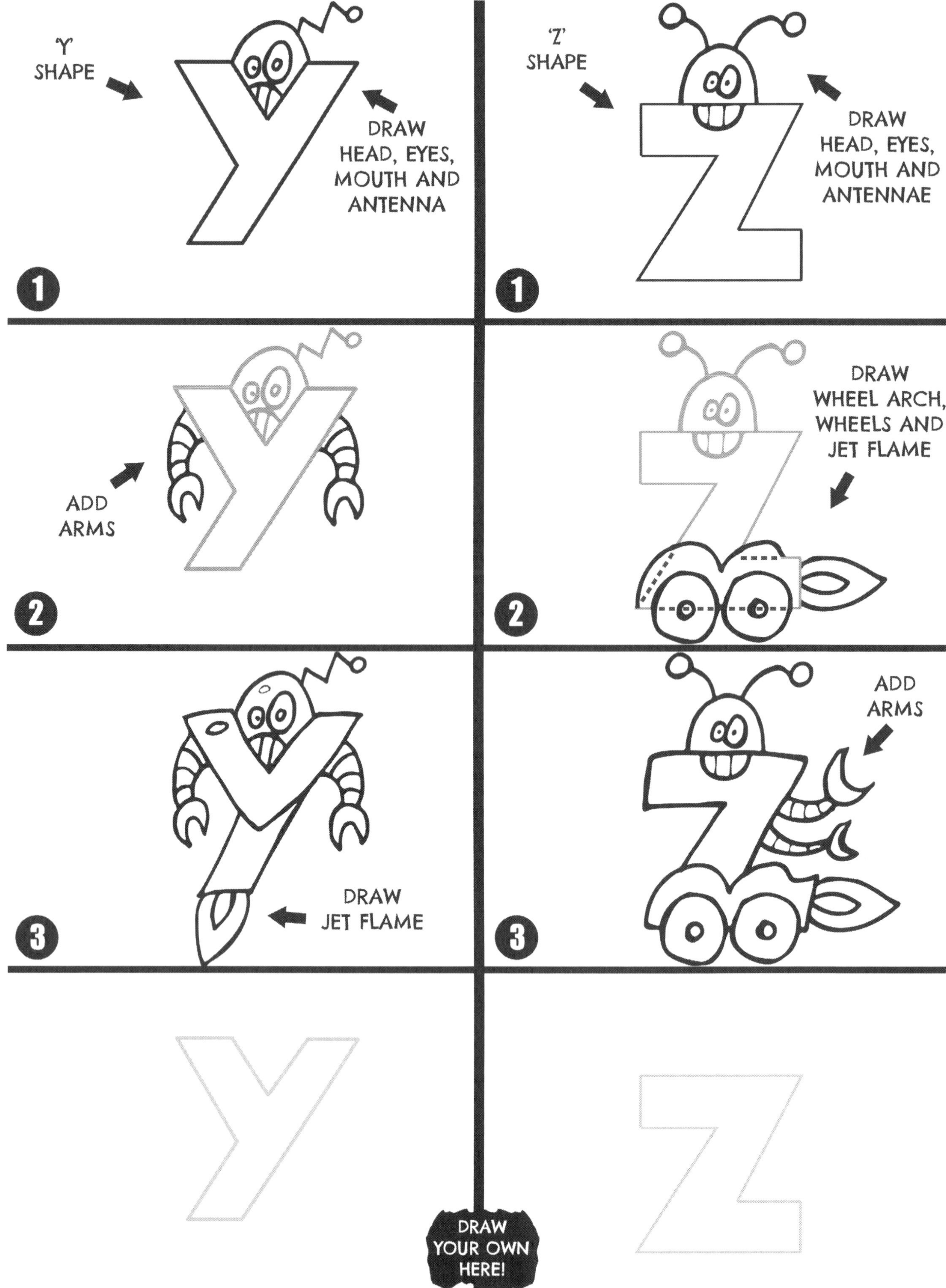
'Y'
SHAPE
DRAW
HEAD, EYES,
MOUTH AND
ANTENNA
'Z'
SHAPE
DRAW
HEAD, EYES,
MOUTH AND
ANTENNAE
1
1
ADD
ARMS
DRAW
WHEEL ARCH,
WHEELS AND
JET FLAME
2
2
DRAW
JET FLAME
ADD
ARMS
3
3
DRAW
YOUR OWN
HERE!

SHAPE
BEASTS

EGG SHAPE
DRAW EYES AND MOUTH
1
EGG SHAPE
ADD EYE AND MOUTH
1
ADD ARMS AND LEGS
2
DRAW FOUR ARMS
2
GIVE IT SOME HAIR
3
ADD HAIR
DRAW LEGS
3
DRAW YOUR OWN HERE!

EGG SHAPE
DRAW EYES, NOSE AND MOUTH
1
EGG SHAPE
DRAW CLOAK COLLAR AND BUTTONS
ADD EYES, MOUTH, EARS AND HAIR
1
ADD ARMS AND LEGS
2
DRAW FEET AND BOTTOM OF THE CLOAK
2
DRAW HORNS
GIVE IT A TAIL
3
DRAW A BAT
ADD ARMS
3
DRAW YOUR OWN HERE!

EGG
SHAPE
DRAW
EYE, MOUTH
AND EYEBROW
1
EGG
SHAPE
ADD
EYE AND
LIPS
1
ADD
ARMS AND
WINGS
2
DRAW FOUR
TENTACLES
2
ADD
HORNS
DRAW
FEET
3
DRAW HEAD
TENTACLES
ADD
SPOTS
ADD
FEET
3
DRAW
YOUR OWN
HERE!

EGG SHAPE
DRAW LOTS OF EYES, AND A MOUTH
1
EGG SHAPE
ADD EYES ON STALKS, AND MOUTH
1
ADD SIX LEGS
2
DRAW TAIL AND SPIKES
2
DRAW EYEBALL ON STALK
3
ADD SPIKES TO NOSE AND BODY
3
DRAW YOUR OWN HERE!

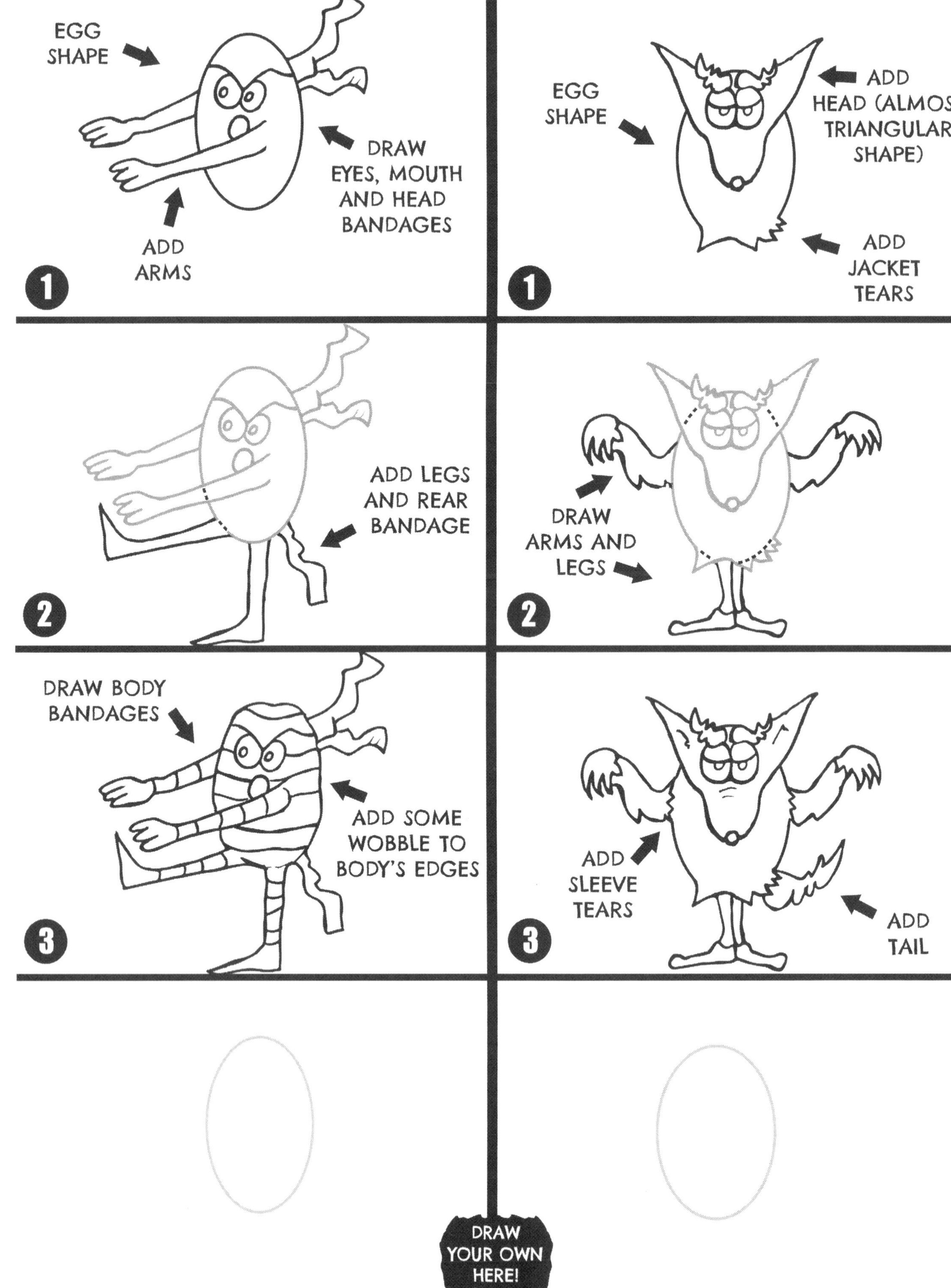
EGG SHAPE
DRAW EYES, MOUTH AND HEAD BANDAGES
ADD ARMS
1
EGG SHAPE
ADD HEAD (ALMOST TRIANGULAR SHAPE)
ADD JACKET TEARS
1
ADD LEGS AND REAR BANDAGE
2
DRAW ARMS AND LEGS
2
DRAW BODY BANDAGES
ADD SOME WOBBLE TO BODY'S EDGES
3
ADD SLEEVE TEARS
ADD TAIL
3
DRAW YOUR OWN HERE!

HALF ROUNDED SQUARE SHAPE
DRAW EYES AND MOUTH
1
HALF ROUNDED SQUARE SHAPE
ADD EYES, MOUTH, NOSTRILS AND BELLYBUTTON
1
ADD HORNS AND FUR TUFTS
2
DRAW EARS AND ARMS
2
DRAW TAIL
ADD FEET
3
ADD TAIL AND FEET
3
DRAW YOUR OWN HERE!

HALF ROUNDED SQUARE SHAPE
DRAW A SECOND HALF ROUNDED SQUARE SHAPE INSIDE
DRAW EYES, CHEEKBONES AND TEETH
1
HALF ROUNDED SQUARE SHAPE
ADD EYE, MOUTH AND SLIME
1
ADD LEGS
2
DRAW SLIMY ARMS
2
DRAW ARMS AND SCYTHE
3
ADD MORE SLIME
3
DRAW YOUR OWN HERE!

HALF ROUNDED SQUARE SHAPE
DRAW EYES, LIPS AND HEAD RIDGES
1
HALF ROUNDED SQUARE SHAPE
ADD EYES, MOUTH AND STITCHES
1
ADD ARMS AND LEGS
2
DRAW ARMS
2
DRAW HEAD FIN AND HAIR
3
ADD LEGS
3
DRAW YOUR OWN HERE!

HALF
ROUNDED
SQUARE
SHAPE
DRAW
EYE, TEETH
AND SPOTS
1
HALF
ROUNDED
SQUARE
SHAPE
ADD
EYES, MOUTH,
NOSTRILS AND
CHEEKBONES
1
DRAW
TAIL
ADD
FEET
2
ADD
HAIR
DRAW
ARMS
2
ADD
HEAD SPIKES
3
ADD
LEGS
3
DRAW
YOUR OWN
HERE!

HALF
ROUNDED
SQUARE
SHAPE
DRAW
EYES, NOSE
AND MOUTH
1
HALF
ROUNDED
SQUARE
SHAPE
ADD
EYES, NOSE,
MOUTH AND
BELLYBUTTON
1
ADD
ARMS
ADD
FEET
2
DRAW
WINGS
ADD
EYEBROWS
DRAW
ARMS
2
DRAW
EARS AND
EYEBROWS
DRAW
TAIL
3
DRAW
FEET
ADD
TAIL
3
DRAW
YOUR OWN
HERE!

SHAPE BOTS

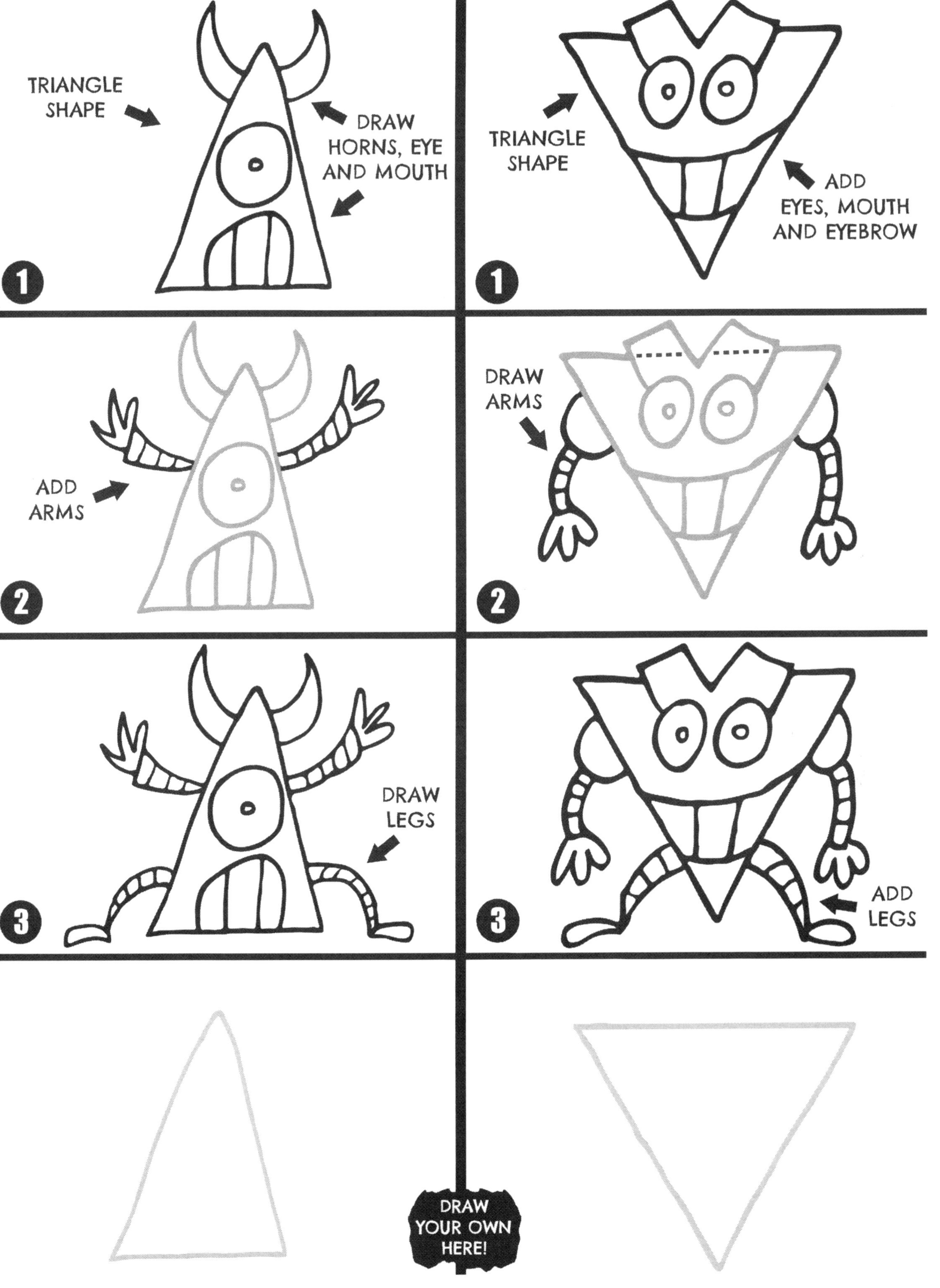
TRIANGLE SHAPE
DRAW HORNS, EYE AND MOUTH
1
TRIANGLE SHAPE
ADD EYES, MOUTH AND EYEBROW
1
ADD ARMS
2
DRAW ARMS
2
DRAW LEGS
3
ADD LEGS
3
DRAW YOUR OWN HERE!

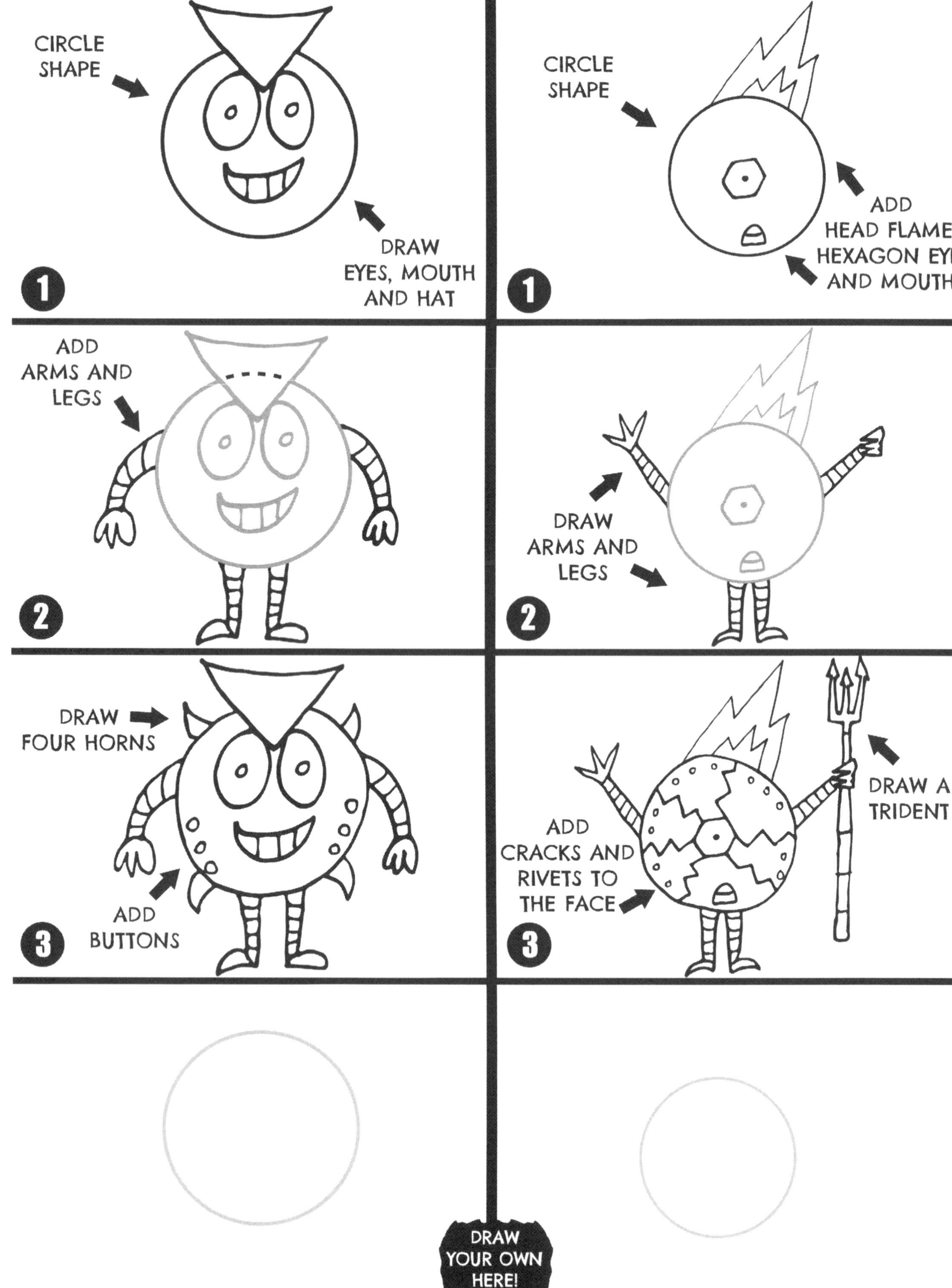
CIRCLE SHAPE
DRAW EYES, MOUTH AND HAT
1
CIRCLE SHAPE
ADD HEAD FLAME, HEXAGON EYE, AND MOUTH
1
ADD ARMS AND LEGS
2
DRAW ARMS AND LEGS
2
DRAW FOUR HORNS
ADD BUTTONS
3
DRAW A TRIDENT
ADD CRACKS AND RIVETS TO THE FACE
3
DRAW YOUR OWN HERE!

SQUARE SHAPE
DRAW EYES, EYEBROW AND NOSE
1
SQUARE SHAPE
ADD EYES, MOUTH AND ARM/LEG SOCKETS
1
ADD ARMS AND LEGS
2
DRAW ARMS
2
DRAW MOUTH AND HORNS
3
ADD LEGS
3
DRAW YOUR OWN HERE!

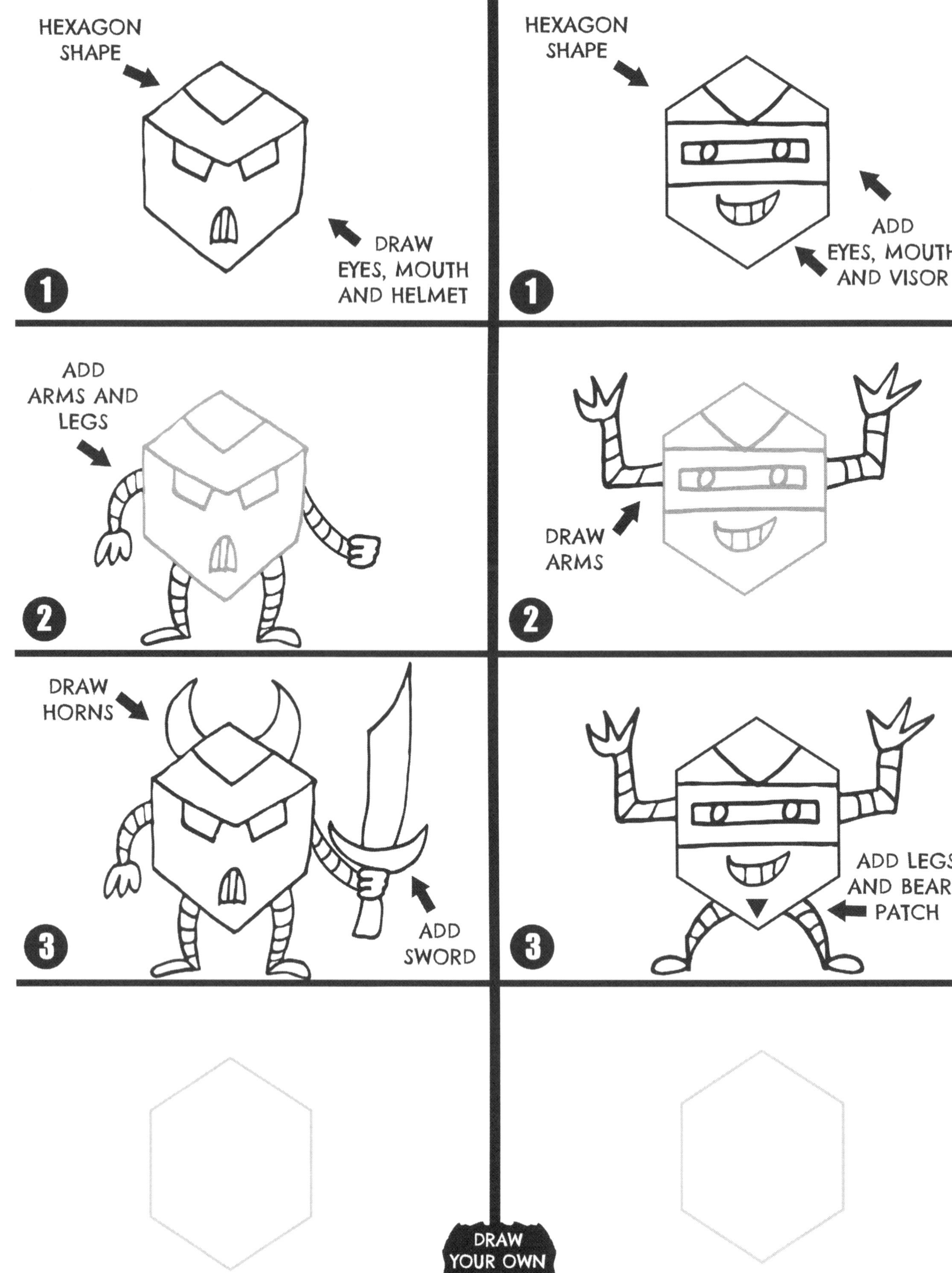
HEXAGON SHAPE
DRAW EYES, MOUTH AND HELMET
1
HEXAGON SHAPE
ADD EYES, MOUTH AND VISOR
1
ADD ARMS AND LEGS
2
DRAW ARMS
2
DRAW HORNS
ADD SWORD
3
ADD LEGS AND BEARD PATCH
3
DRAW YOUR OWN HERE!

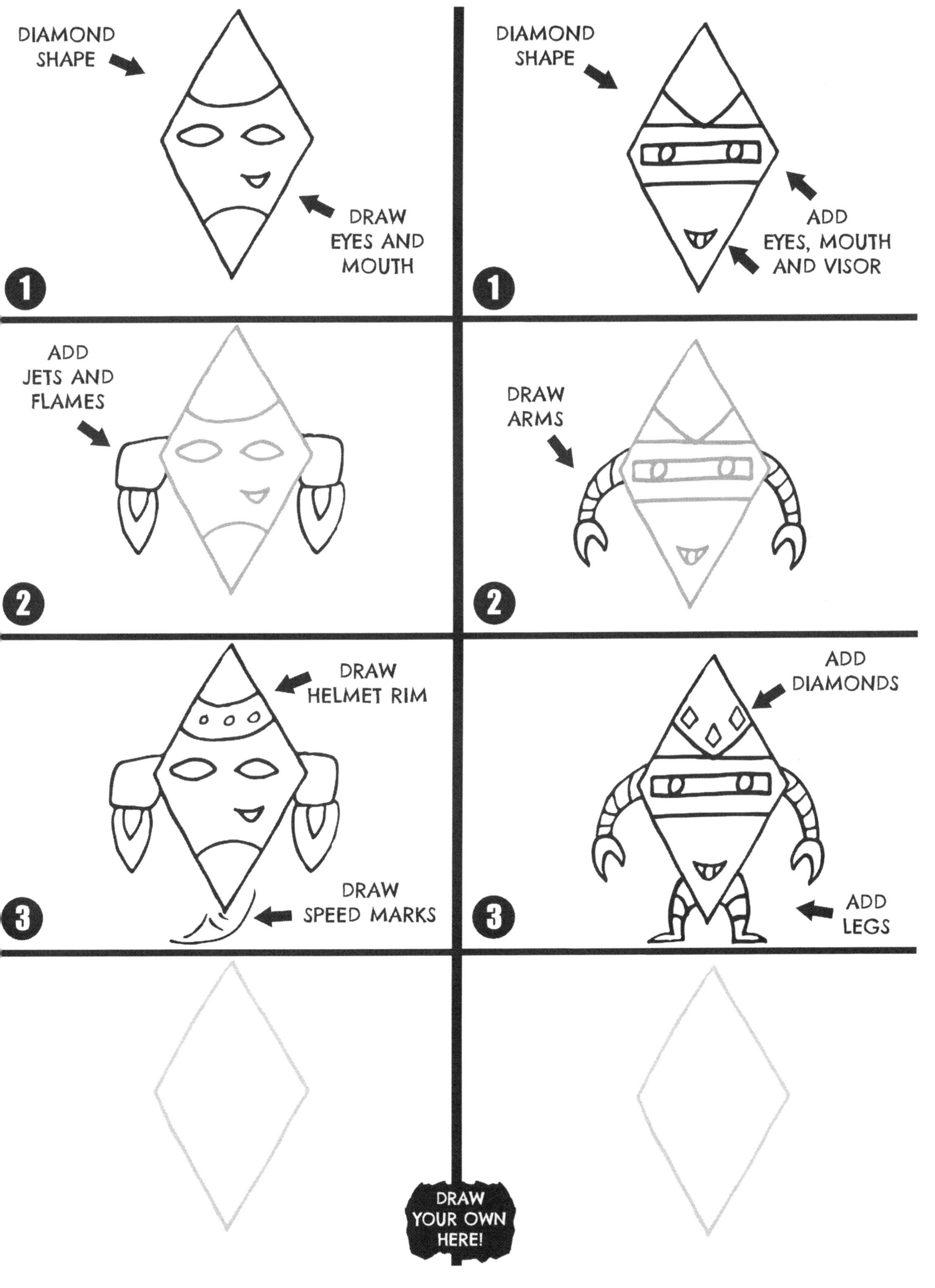
DIAMOND SHAPE
DRAW EYES AND MOUTH
1
DIAMOND SHAPE
ADD EYES, MOUTH AND VISOR
1
ADD JETS AND FLAMES
2
DRAW ARMS
2
DRAW HELMET RIM
DRAW SPEED MARKS
3
ADD DIAMONDS
ADD LEGS
3
DRAW YOUR OWN HERE!

HALF ROUNDED RECTANGLE SHAPE
DRAW ANTENNAE, MOUTH, EYEBALL AND VISOR
1
HALF ROUNDED RECTANGLE SHAPE
ADD EYES, MOUTH AND VISOR
1
ADD ARMS
2
DRAW ARMS
2
DRAW LEGS
3
ADD AERIALS
ADD LEGS
3
DRAW YOUR OWN HERE!

HALF ROUNDED RECTANGLE SHAPE
DRAW HORNS, EYES AND TEETH
1
HALF ROUNDED RECTANGLE SHAPE
ADD EYES, MOUTH AND HAT
1
ADD ARMS
2
DRAW ARMS
2
DRAW LEGS AND TAIL
3
ADD LEGS
3
DRAW YOUR OWN HERE!

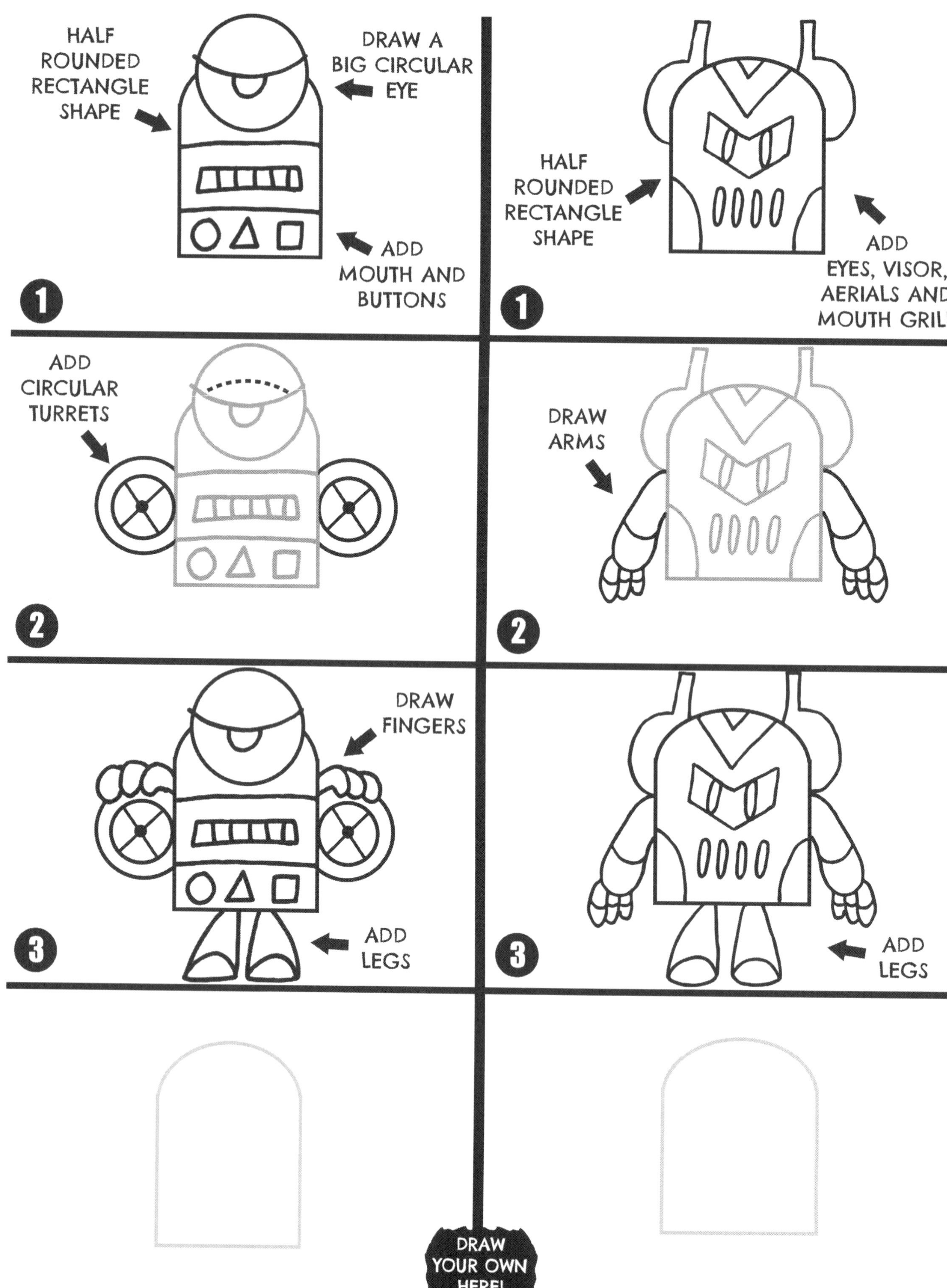
HALF ROUNDED RECTANGLE SHAPE
DRAW A BIG CIRCULAR EYE
ADD MOUTH AND BUTTONS
1
HALF ROUNDED RECTANGLE SHAPE
ADD EYES, VISOR, AERIALS AND MOUTH GRILL
1
ADD CIRCULAR TURRETS
2
DRAW ARMS
2
DRAW FINGERS
ADD LEGS
3
ADD LEGS
3
DRAW YOUR OWN HERE!

HALF ROUNDED SQUARE SHAPE
DRAW EYES, MOUTH AND EYEBROW
1
HALF ROUNDED SQUARE SHAPE
ADD EYES, MOUTH AND SPIKES
1
ADD ARMS
2
DRAW ARMS
2
3
DRAW LEGS
3
ADD LEGS
DRAW YOUR OWN HERE!

HALF ROUNDED SQUARE SHAPE
DRAW AERIAL, EYES, MOUTH AND CHEEK BONES
1
HALF ROUNDED SQUARE SHAPE
ADD EYES, NOSE, MOUTH AND SPIKES
1
ADD ARMS
2
DRAW ARMS
2
DRAW LEGS
3
ADD LEGS
3
DRAW YOUR OWN HERE!

COSTUME BEASTS
& WOBBLE BOTS

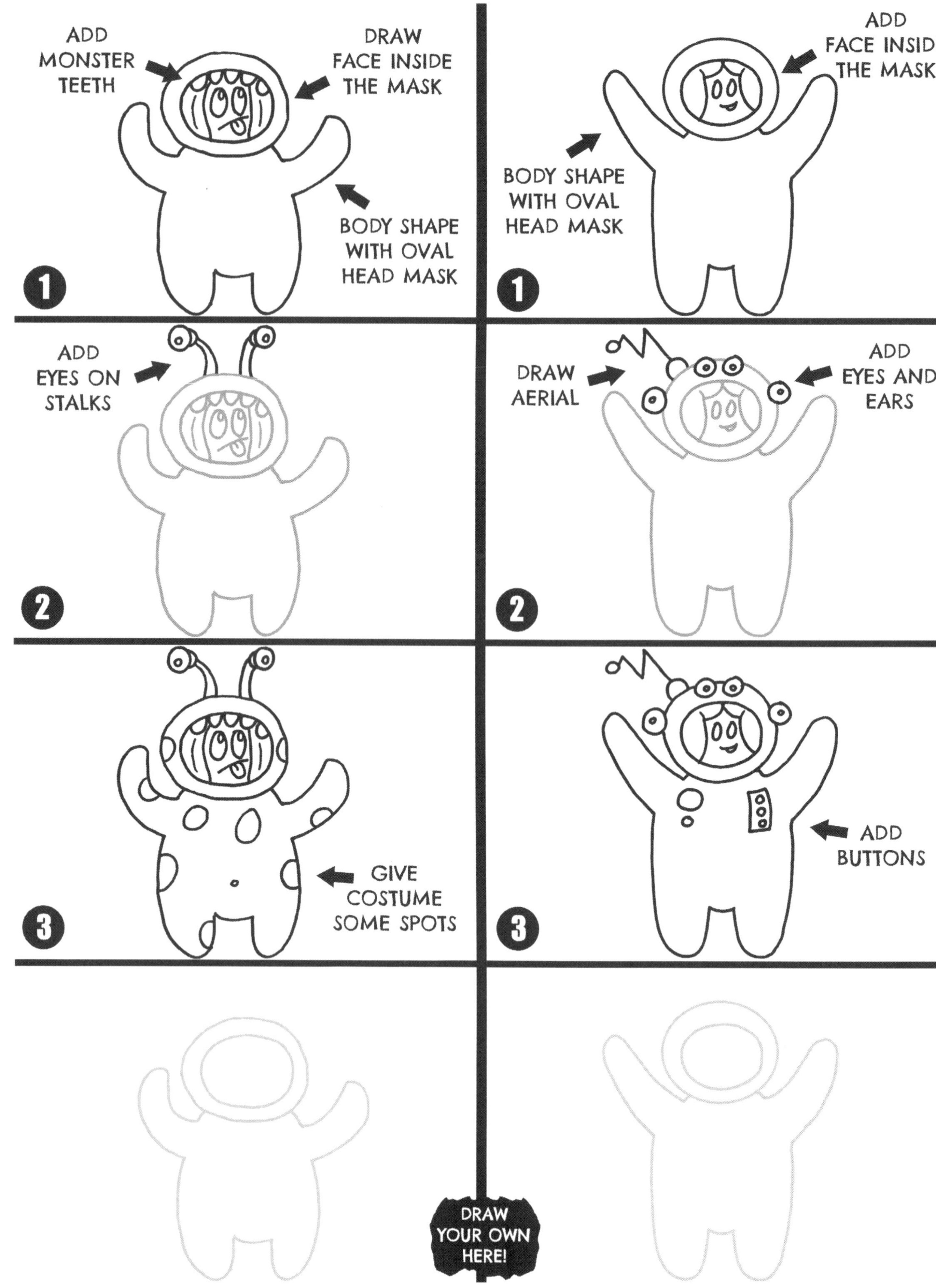
ADD MONSTER TEETH
DRAW FACE INSIDE THE MASK
BODY SHAPE WITH OVAL HEAD MASK
1
ADD FACE INSIDE THE MASK
BODY SHAPE WITH OVAL HEAD MASK
1
ADD EYES ON STALKS
2
DRAW AERIAL
ADD EYES AND EARS
2
GIVE COSTUME SOME SPOTS
3
ADD BUTTONS
3
DRAW YOUR OWN HERE!

DRAW FACE INSIDE MASK, AND MONSTER TEETH
BODY SHAPE WITH TAIL AND OVAL HEAD MASK
1
ADD FACE INSIDE MASK, AND MONSTER TEETH
BODY SHAPE WITH OVAL HEAD MASK
1
DRAW EYES, NOSTRILS AND HEAD SPIKES
ADD TAIL SPIKES
ADD CLAWS
2
DRAW EYES, EARS AND HAIR
2
ADD SPOTS
3
ADD CAPE
3
DRAW YOUR OWN HERE!

ROUNDED SQUARE HEAD MASK
DRAW FACE INSIDE MASK, AND MONSTER TEETH
1
ADD NECK FUR TO OVAL HEAD MASK
DRAW FACE INSIDE MASK, AND MONSTER NOSE AND TEETH
1
ADD NECK BOLTS
ADD EYES AND STITCHES TO MASK
2
DRAW EARS, HAIR AND EYES
ADD TAIL
2
GIVE THE COSTUME A FEW MORE STITCHES
3
ADD BUTTONS AND TEARS TO COSTUME
3
DRAW YOUR OWN HERE!

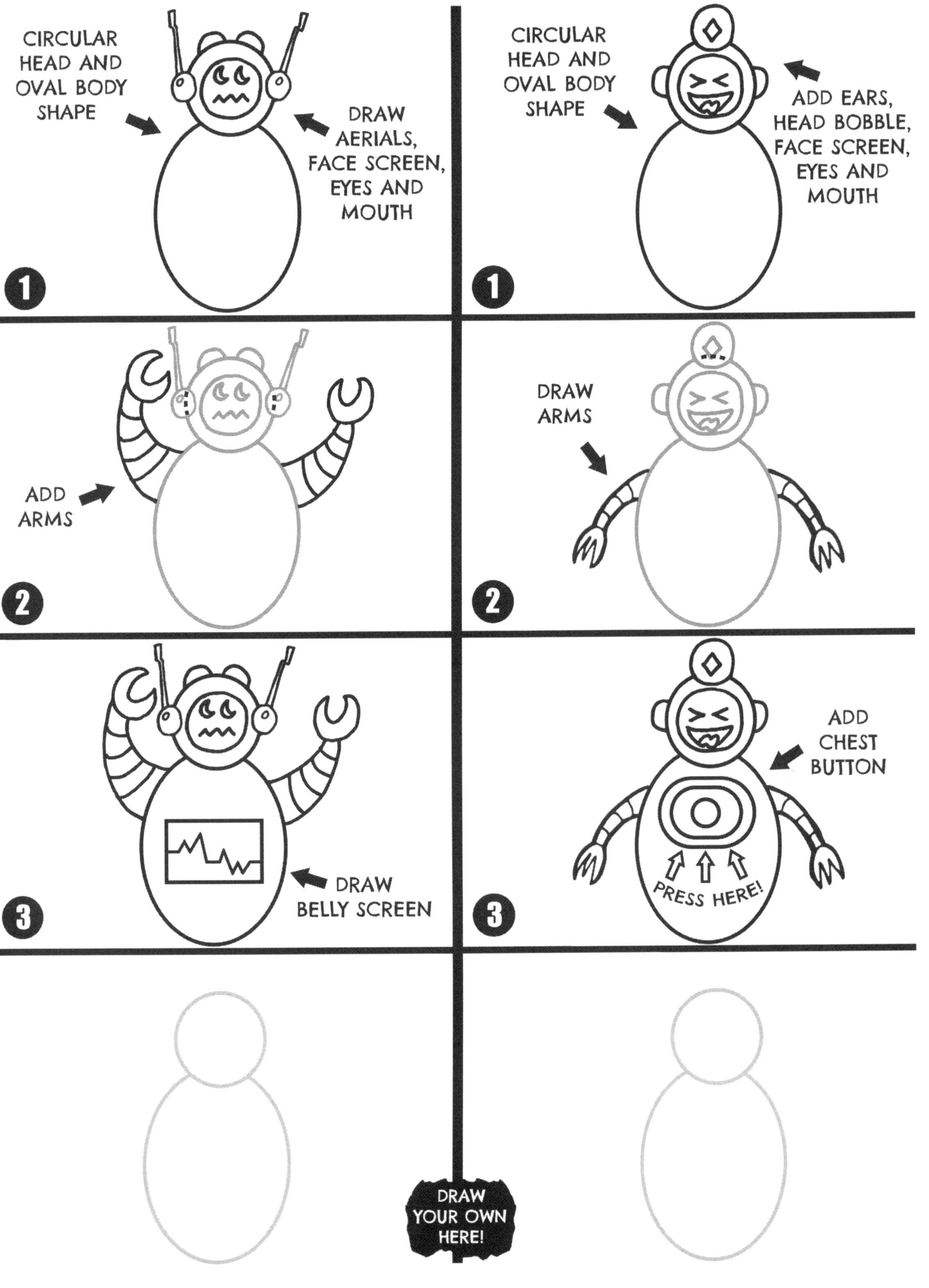
CIRCULAR HEAD AND OVAL BODY SHAPE
DRAW AERIALS, FACE SCREEN, EYES AND MOUTH
1
CIRCULAR HEAD AND OVAL BODY SHAPE
ADD EARS, HEAD BOBBLE, FACE SCREEN, EYES AND MOUTH
1
ADD ARMS
2
DRAW ARMS
2
DRAW BELLY SCREEN
3
ADD CHEST BUTTON
PRESS HERE!
3
DRAW YOUR OWN HERE!

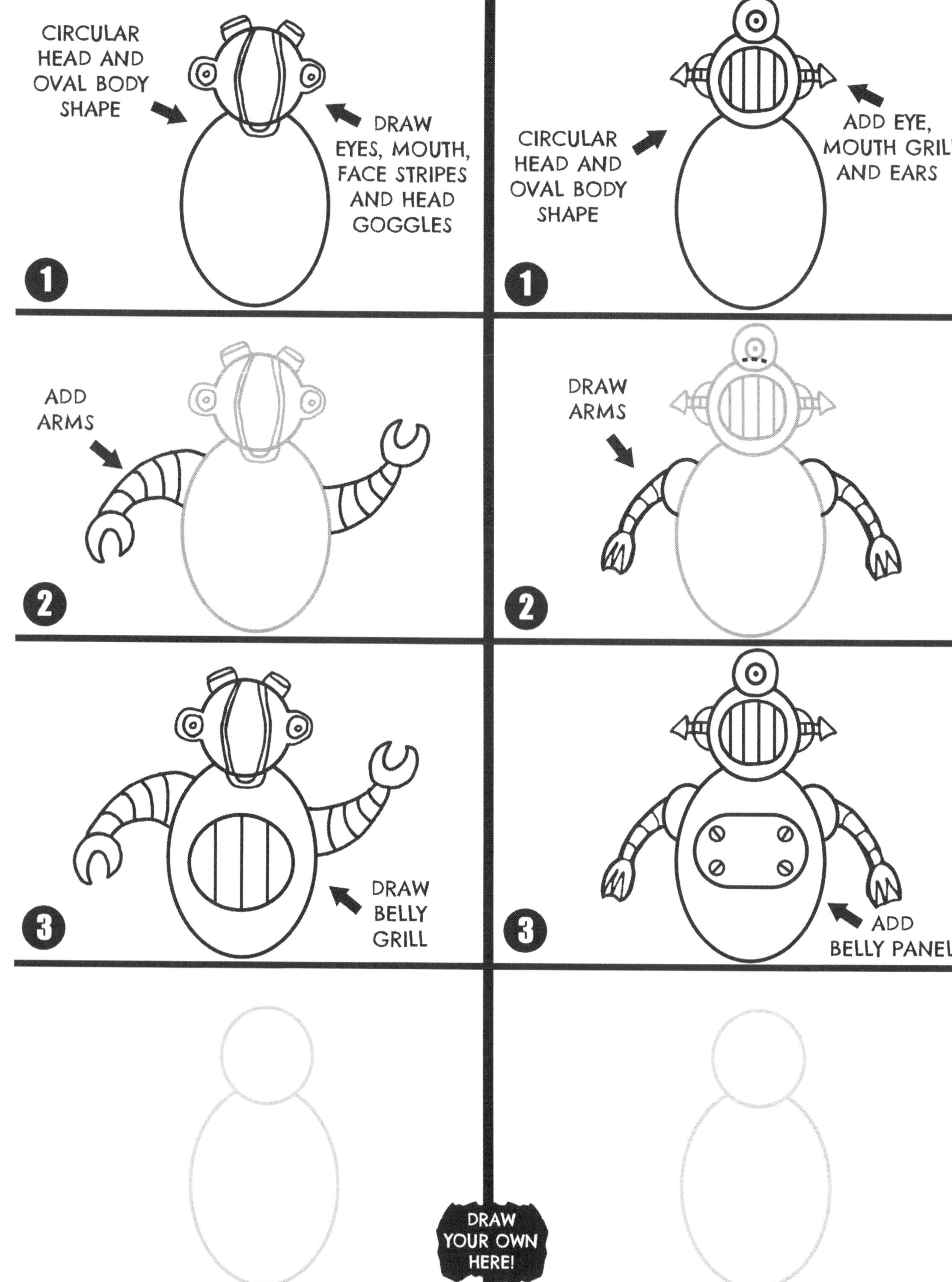
CIRCULAR HEAD AND OVAL BODY SHAPE
DRAW EYES, MOUTH, FACE STRIPES AND HEAD GOGGLES
1
CIRCULAR HEAD AND OVAL BODY SHAPE
ADD EYE, MOUTH GRILL AND EARS
1
ADD ARMS
2
DRAW ARMS
2
DRAW BELLY GRILL
3
ADD BELLY PANEL
3
DRAW YOUR OWN HERE!

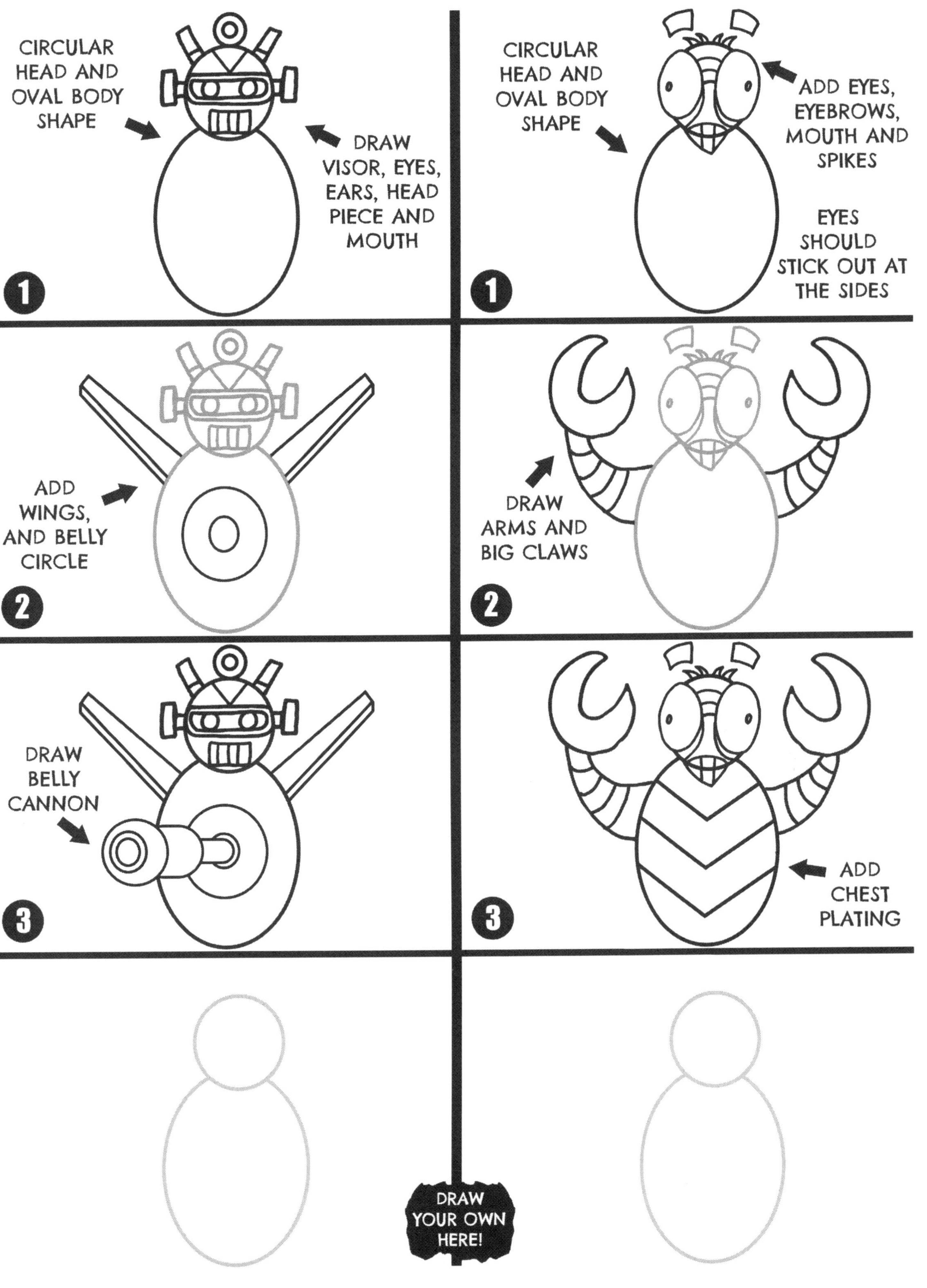
CIRCULAR HEAD AND OVAL BODY SHAPE
DRAW VISOR, EYES, EARS, HEAD PIECE AND MOUTH
1
CIRCULAR HEAD AND OVAL BODY SHAPE
ADD EYES, EYEBROWS, MOUTH AND SPIKES
EYES SHOULD STICK OUT AT THE SIDES
1
ADD WINGS, AND BELLY CIRCLE
2
DRAW ARMS AND BIG CLAWS
2
DRAW BELLY CANNON
3
ADD CHEST PLATING
3
DRAW YOUR OWN HERE!

SECTION TWO
CREATE YOUR OWN COMIC!

GREETINGS, AND WELCOME TO THE COMIC CREATION SECTION - OVERFLOWING WITH EMPTY COMIC PANELS JUST WAITING TO BE FILLED!
WHEN CREATING A COMIC THE ONLY LIMIT IS YOUR IMAGINATION.
EITHER CREATE YOUR VERY OWN CHARACTERS TO USE IN YOUR COMIC, OR USE THE ONES PROVIDED IN THE FIRST SECTION.

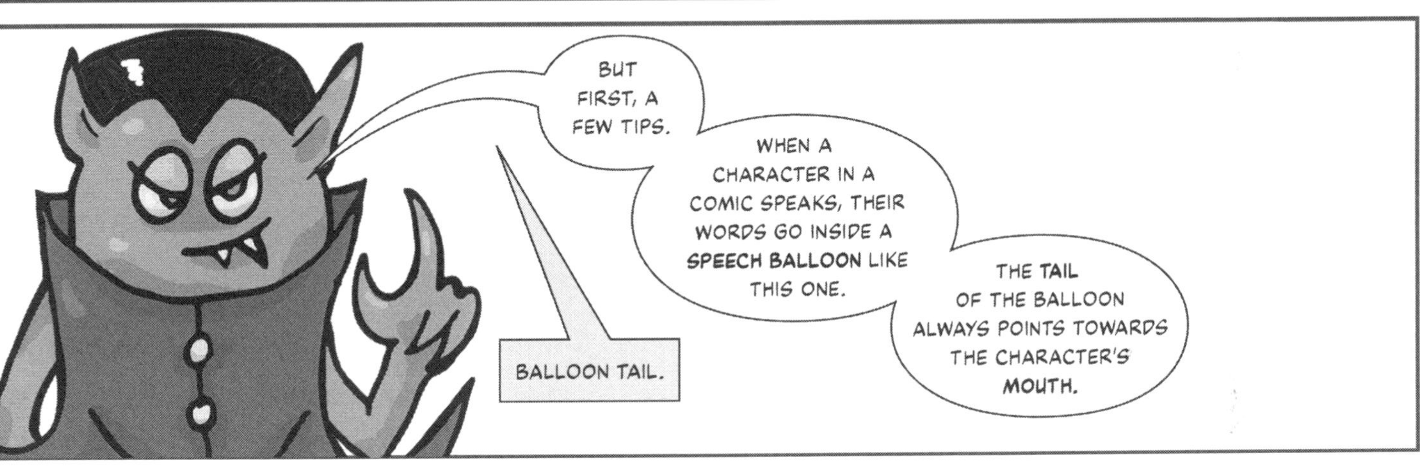
BUT FIRST, A FEW TIPS.
WHEN A CHARACTER IN A COMIC SPEAKS, THEIR WORDS GO INSIDE A **SPEECH BALLOON** LIKE THIS ONE.
THE **TAIL** OF THE BALLOON ALWAYS POINTS TOWARDS THE CHARACTER'S **MOUTH.**
BALLOON TAIL.

MEANWHILE, IN A SECRET ROBOTICS LAB...
BEEP BOOP! CAPTION BOXES LIKE THE ONE ABOVE CAN BE USED TO GIVE READERS **IMPORTANT INFORMATION**, SUCH AS A CHANGE OF LOCATION BETWEEN PANELS.

LEAP!
AND DON'T FORGET TO THROW IN SOME **SOUND EFFECTS**, ESPECIALLY IF IT'S A FIGHT SCENE!
BOF!

ONE LAST THING BEFORE YOU GET STARTED... NO COMIC IS COMPLETE WITHOUT AN EYE CATCHING COVER.
THE COVER IS SPLIT INTO THREE SECTIONS.
BEASTLY COMIX
MONSTERS VS ROBOTS!
1 LOGO.
2 TITLE.
3 MAIN IMAGE.
TEST A FEW OF YOUR COVER DESIGN IDEAS BELOW, BEFORE YOU DRAW THE FINAL ONE ON THE NEXT PAGE.

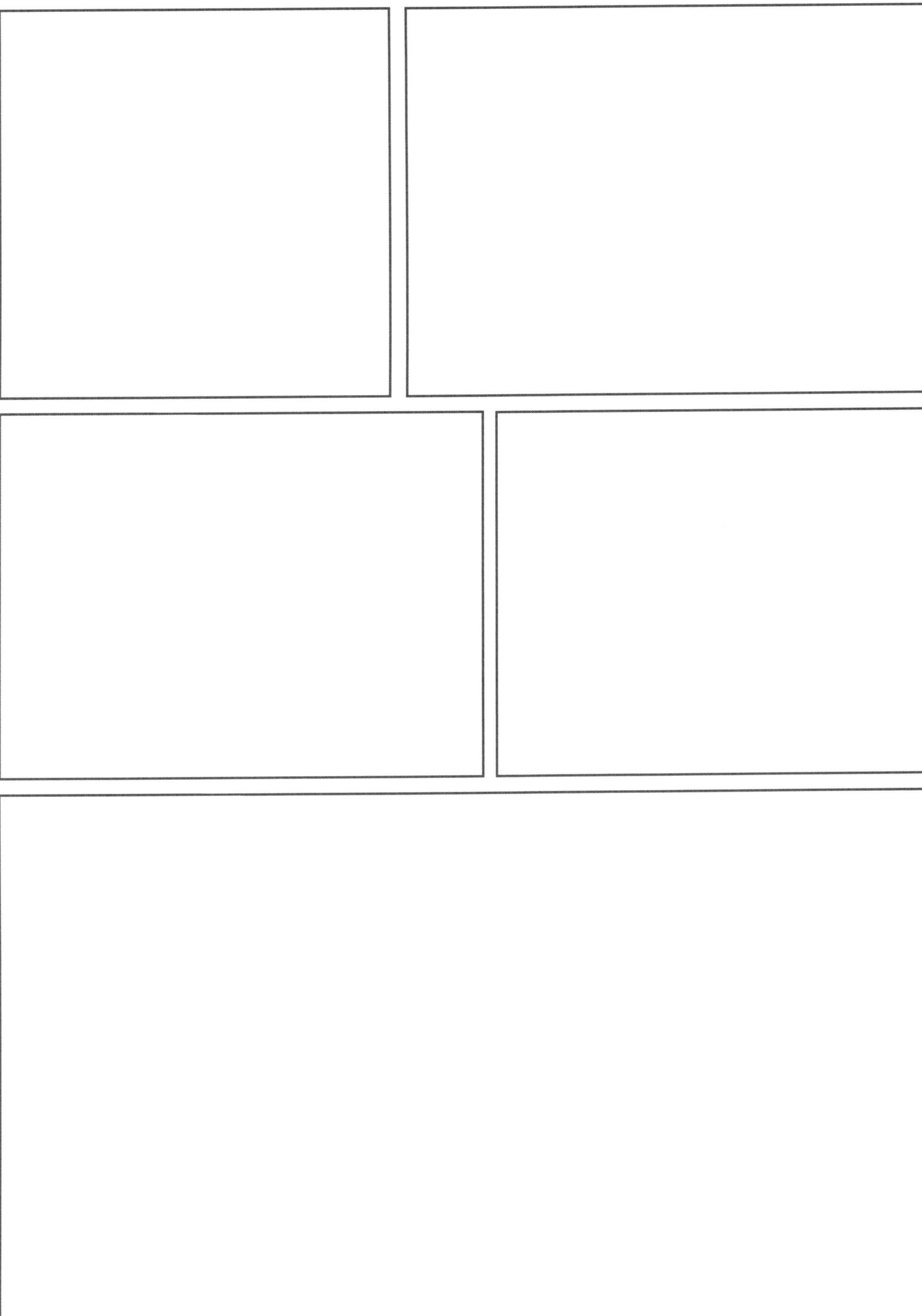

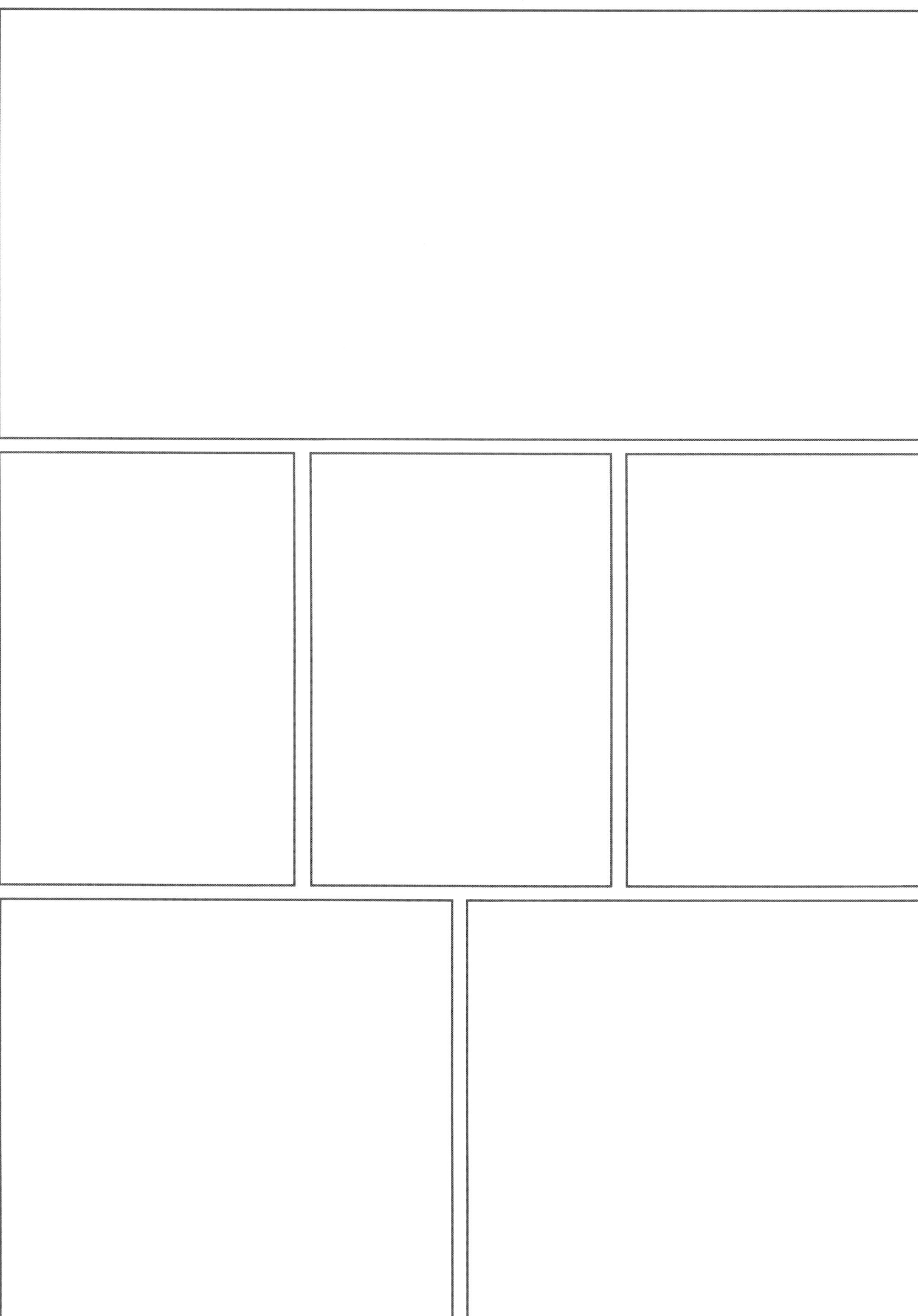

Yum Yum
By Angus
Shark

dinasor

Printed in Great Britain
by Amazon

12073326R00063